Current Issues in Administrative Law

Current Issues in Administrative Law

Edited by

Cătălin-Silviu Săraru

Cambridge Scholars Publishing

Current Issues in Administrative Law

Edited by Cătălin-Silviu Săraru

This book first published 2020

Cambridge Scholars Publishing

Lady Stephenson Library, Newcastle upon Tyne, NE6 2PA, UK

British Library Cataloguing in Publication Data
A catalogue record for this book is available from the British Library

ISBN (10): 1-5275-5552-6
ISBN (13): 978-1-5275-5552-5

TABLE OF CONTENTS

PREFACE

ASSOCIATE PROFESSOR CĂTĂLIN-SILVIU SĂRARU, EDITOR

DEPARTMENT OF LAW, BUCHAREST UNIVERSITY OF ECONOMIC STUDIES

This volume contains a selection of scientific papers presented at the Ninth International Conference on Perspectives of Business Law in the Third Millennium. This conference was held on 8 November 2019 at Bucharest University of Economic Studies, Romania. Each year, the conference is organized by the Department of Law at Bucharest University of Economic Studies together with the Society of Juridical and Administrative Sciences. More information about the conference can be found on the official website: www.businesslawconference.ro.

The scientific studies included in this volume are grouped into three parts:

- *Reconfiguration of administrative law from the perspective of redefining social action and public interest in the "state of law".* The papers in this chapter deal with the "state of law" in theory and reality, focusing on social action in legal perspective, in terms of its relationship and public interest, and the challenges and possibilities in identifying the content of this notion.
- *Administrative codification in comparative law.* This chapter includes papers on: deconcentrated public services according to the Administrative Code and legal aspects of electronic communication according to its regulation in the Administrative Procedure Code.
- *Contemporary challenges in European and comparative administrative law.* The papers in this chapter deal with a number of issues. These include: the principle of revocation in Romanian administrative law, being an exception regarding administrative acts that have entered the civil circuit and produced legal effects;

the validity of tender proposals and of guaranteeing participation in terms of the will of the contracting authority and that of the bidder with a synthesis of the relevant case law in public procurement; challenges and perspectives on the evolution of Romanian administrative litigation; identifying the right of petition in the Romanian Constitution, the Moldovan Constitution, and in comparative law; a comparative analysis of the concepts of personal data and protection in the context of border procedures (Ukraine, European Union); and the historic decision of the Court of Justice of the European Union on the obligation of member states to recognize university degrees obtained through simultaneous study.

This volume is aimed at practitioners, researchers, students, and PhD candidates in juridical sciences who are interested in recent developments and prospects for development in the field of administrative law at the national and international levels.

We gratefully acknowledge the support of the *Society of Juridical and Administrative Sciences (Societatea de Stiinte Juridice si Administrative)*, Bucharest.

We thank all contributors and partners and are confident that this volume will meet the growing need for documentation and information among readers in the context of globalization and contemporary administrative law.

About the Editor Cătălin-Silviu Săraru

Activity
Cătălin-Silviu Săraru, PhD, is an associate professor in the Law Department of Bucharest University of Economic Studies, specializing in national and European administrative law and administrative contract law. He is an arbitrator at the Court of International Commercial Arbitration (Romania); a lawyer of the Bucharest Bar Association; and the editor in chief of the journal *Juridical Tribune: Tribuna Juridica* (indexed in Clarivate Analytics) and *Perspectives of Law and Public Administration*. He is also a member of the editorial board of several scientific journals, including: *International Law Research (ILR)* (Toronto, Canada), *the Journal of Legal Studies*, *the Journal of Law and Administrative Sciences*, *Dreptul*, and *Acta Universitatis Danubius. Juridica, Reflecții Academice*. He is president of the *Society of Juridical and Administrative Sciences* and a member of the *Société de législation comparée*, the *Research Network on EU Administrative Law* (ReNEUAL), the *Union of Jurists of Romania*, and the *Institute of Administrative Sciences "Paul Negulescu"*.

Publications
Cătălin-Silviu Săraru is the editor of two volumes: *Contemporary Challenges in Business Law* (ADJURIS International Academic Publisher, 2016); *Studies in Business Law—Recent Developments and Perspectives* (Peter Lang International Academic Publishers, 2013). He is the sole author of ten books including: *Drept administrativ. Probleme fundamentale ale dreptului public* (*Administrative law. Fundamental issues of public law*, C. H. Beck Publishing House, Bucharest, 2016); *Legea contenciosului administrativ nr. 554/2004. Examen critic al Deciziilor Curtii Constitutionale* (*Administrative Litigation Law no. 554/2004. Critical examination of Constitutional Court decisions*, C. H. Beck Publishing House, Bucharest, 2015); *Contractele administrative. Reglementare, doctrină, jurisprudență* (*Administrative agreements. Regulatory, doctrine, jurisprudence*, C. H. Beck Publishing House, Bucharest, 2009). He is coauthor of two books, including *Drept administrativ European* (*European Administrative Law*, Lumina Lex Publishing House, Bucharest, 2005) and the author of more

than 100 journal articles published in: *Juridical Tribune: Tribuna Juridica, the Transylvanian Review of Administrative Sciences, Acta Juridica Hungarica, Dreptul, Juridical Current, Acta Universitatis Danubius. Juridica, Revista de Drept Public, Pandectele române, Curierul Judiciar, Notebooks of international law*, and *Tribuna Economică, Economie și Administrație locală.*

Prizes

He was awarded the "Anibal Teodorescu" Prize by the Union of Jurists of Romania in 2014 for the work "Cartea de contracte administrative: modele, comentarii, explicații" (The Book of administrative contracts: models, comments, explanations, C. H. Beck Publishing House, Bucharest, 2013).

PART I.

RECONFIGURATION OF ADMINISTRATIVE LAW FROM THE PERSPECTIVE OF REDEFINING SOCIAL ACTION AND PUBLIC INTEREST IN THE "STATE OF LAW"

The State of Law: Between Theory and Reality

PhD. Student Raluca TOMESCU[1]

Abstract: *Not just a creation of the modern world, such phrases as the "rule of law" or the "state of law" are found in post-December Revolution (1989) law dictionaries and give us a new conceptual perspective on the institution of the state. These concepts have been transposed into the phrase the "rule of law", as evident in article 1 paragraph 3 of the Constitution of Romania, establishing that "Romania is a democratic and social state, governed by the rule of law". Among the 130 paradigms of the word "right" offered by The Explanatory Dictionary of the Romanian Language, we may consider adding one more—the one that defines a state whose legal system is based on the four validated principles of the concept of the "rule of law". These are: the supremacy of the constitution; the guarantee of the security and constitutional rights of citizens; civil society as an equal partner of the state; and the separation of state powers. State power is shared between different institutional compartments (legislative, executive, and judiciary) with separate and independent powers and responsibilities. Legislative power, as well as democracy itself, is related to a country's recognition of its constitutional rights and principles, developing from a simple institutional basis and becoming a "state" under the "rule of law". This article proposes a debate on the meaning that the legislature wished to give to the notion of the "rule of law", in terms of the principles of its underlying concept as expressed in the articles of the Romanian Constitution. As such, The Explanatory Dictionary of the Romanian Language may be lacking a new paradigm of the word "right", seeing rather the presence of a pleonasm.*

Keywords: *state of law, constitution, law, state.*

JEL Classification: K00, K10

---

[1] Raluca Tomescu: Nicolae Titulescu University, Bucharest, Romania, ratomescu@gmail.com.

1. Introductory considerations

The phrase "state of law" is becoming more and more commonplace. It is heard in the speeches of authority figures and debates in the media; in the speeches of human rights defenders; and especially in the fight against corruption. Yet, looking for a well-defined definition of this phrase, one may easily come to the conclusion that it does not exist. The doctrine provides us with enough material to understand the concept, but what we call a lawful state is still awaiting confirmation.

On the one hand, we have the state, which presents itself as a notion with a double meaning, and on the other hand we have the term *drept* (law). *Drept* is a word with more than a hundred paradigms, but we have some questions, prompting us to make a closer analysis of this term as it is found in the Romanian Constitution.

Romania's Basic Law states in art. 1 paragraph 3 that "*Romania is a democratic and social state, governed by the rule of law*". To this premise, the legislature has added a number of features of the Romanian state, being a state: "*in which human dignity, the citizen's rights and freedoms, the free development of human personality, justice and political pluralism represent supreme values, in the spirit of the democratic traditions of the Romanian people and the ideals of the Revolution of December 1989, and shall be guaranteed. (4) The State shall be organized based on the principle of the separation and balance of powers—legislative, executive and judicial—within the framework of constitutional democracy. (5) In Romania, the supremacy of the Constitution and the observance of the Constitution and the laws shall be mandatory*". Further, article 16 (1) states "*Citizens are equal before the law and the public authorities, with no privileges and with no discrimination. (2) No one is above the law*".

Clearly, the legislature's vision of a "state of law" is not sufficient to grasp that democratic, social, and human dignity, the rights and freedoms of citizens, the free development of one's personality, and human justice and political pluralism stand for supreme values guaranteed to all. The State has to be organized on the principle of the separation and balance of powers so that citizens enjoy equality in the face of the law and the public authorities and no one is above the law. Individually listing each of these characteristics constitutes a pleonasm and it is clear that they are not included in the vision of the legislature as key parts of the "state of law", otherwise there is no reason to repeat them.

Apparently a simple utterance, the phrase "state of law" leads to extensive arguments about its doctrine. The problem of how to define "the state of law" has been the subject of a number of approaches, especially since it has often proved to express a wish, rather than be a reality.

On the one hand, "the state of law" can be regarded as a legal ideology, since the creation of this phrase may suppose that "law" is not considered essential to the state. On the other hand, "*it has been shown that it is difficult, if not impossible to set a boundary between the state and the law, because only a state can be "lawful*"[2]. Starting from these aspects, we aim to analyze and interpret each term individually, in terms of the complete phrase itself, but also in terms of the conceptual character that is at the basis of this lexical creation.

2. The state of law

Firstly, it should be noted that the phrase "state of law" has no etymology in Romanian, this association being incorporated in a complicated doctrinal fashion and representing, in fact, a translation of a concept already established in other states. In this phrase, there are two aspects to be noted: on the one hand, "the law" as a normative concept and on the other, "the state" as an ideological concept. These two aspects have always formed an assemblage combining the part and the whole: "*the state and the law are widely connected, and mutually supportive. They appeared at the same time and for the same reasons and can be explained much better when taken together. The state creates the law and paradoxically, the law delimits the configuration and the actions of the state*"[3].

The normative term "of law" can be presumed to refer primarily to "*all the rules provided and guaranteed by the state, aimed at organizing and disciplining human behavior in major relationships in society in a specific climate manifesting the coexistence of freedoms, defending essential human rights and social justice*"[4].

In the field of ideology, the state can be seen as a product of human society, being "*the legal formula for the organization and existence of a society, people or nation*"[5]. Thus, we may naturally ask the question as to whether the "rule of law" represents "*a legal formula for the organization and existence of a society, people or nation, in which a set of rules, aimed at organizing and disciplining human behavior in the main relations of society, in a specific climate of manifesting the coexistence of freedoms, the*

[2] Steluţa Ionescu, *Justiţia şi marile doctrine privind statul de drept*, "Studii de Drept Românesc", Year 20 (53), No. 1–2, 2008, p. 107–126.
[3] Muraru I, E. S. Tănăsescu, *Drept constituţional şi instituţii politice*, XIII edition, vol.1, C.H. Beck Publishing House, Bucharest, 2008, p.11
[4] Nicolae Popa, *Teoria generală a dreptului*, Bucharest, 1993.
[5] *Idem*, p. 3.

defense of the essential human rights and social justice are assured and guaranteed by the state".

In order to answer this question, and seeking especially to understand the meaning of this phrase, I consider it appropriate to investigate how the notion of state of law is presented in the specialized literature on jurisprudence.

Representing a doctrine in continental European legal thinking, "the state of law" has its roots in German jurisprudence. Opinions of theoreticians on this concept are divided. Some hold that "the state of law" has purely formal features and that, despite its widespread use, the state of law remains "a very elusive concept"[6], being a pleonasm and a legal nonsense. But, on the other hand, there are contrary opinions holding that the state of law corresponds to an anthropological necessity or postulate, and perhaps even an axiom.

In the juridical literature, it is stated that the concept of the state of law might represent "*a constitutional reality whose foundation is to be found within the mechanisms of exercising state power, in the relations between power and the freedom of every individual of the society and the principle of legality in the entire business of the state, but also in the behaviour of each member of society*"[7].

Beyond such polemics, however, the origins of this concept are assumed to be found in ancient principles, similar to those they represent today, and in the diverse contexts of ancient Greece and China, Mesopotamia, India, and Rome. Aristotle famously stated that between a king ruling at his discretion and a king led by the law, the latter would prove to be superior. Cicero is also often quoted, having stated at one point that: "*We are all servants of the law in order to be free*"[8].

As an ideology, the identity of this concept began to take shape in the seventeenth and eighteenth centuries with revolutions in Western countries directed against feudal arbitrariness, "*the idea of the ruling law, another foundation of the issuance of the written constitution, was born also*

---

[6] Tamanaha, Brian Z., *As for the rule of law*, Cambridge University Press, 2004, p. 3.

[7] Marius Andreescu, Claudia Andreescu, *Statul de drept. Semnificații constituționale și jurisprudențiale contemporane*, "Revista Universul Juridic", June 2019.

[8] This is extended: "The magistrates who administer the law, the judges who act as its spokesmen, all those who live as its servants, grant it our loyalty as a guarantee of our freedom." Cicero, *Procese de crimă*, Penguin Classics, Michael Grant. 1975, Harmondsworthp, p. 217. Latin original: "Legum ministri magistratus, legum interpretes iudices, legum denique idcirco omnes servi sumus ut liberi esse possimus", "Pro Cluentio".

in English constitutional practice, considering that the state authorities must respect the pre-established rule of law and consider it, as long as it is not repealed, as sacred"[9].

Albert Dicey theorized the character of Britain in the Victorian age. Conceptually, this had its origins deeply rooted in the past and foreign scholars such as Voltaire, de Lome, de Tocquville, and Gneist all admired the United Kingdom for its respect of the supremacy of law. In 1885, Dicey stated that the *rule of law* was a fundamental pillar of a modern society, based on the equality of law for everyone, with no one punished unless they breached a law, and the individual leaned on the constitution[10].

Jaques Chevallier defines the "state of law", in a very pragmatic and clear manner, as "the *kind of political regime in which the power of the state is framed and limited by the law*".

At the end of the nineteenth century, the German juridical doctrine "*Rechtsstaat*" or "state of law" appeared. Its source, from which the development of this juridical theory departed, was the Kantian approach to civil society[11]. The "state of law" appears similar to that of the "constitutional state" in which the exercise of governmental power is constrained by the law. Thus the "state of law" appears conceptually opposed to *Obrigkeitsstaat* or *Nichtrechtsstaat* (a state based on the arbitrary use of power) and *Unrechtsstaat* (a non-*Rechtsstaat* with the possibility of developing into one after a period of historical development).

Later, this complicated doctrine was adopted into the French doctrine of "était et droit", gradually becoming a general term across the entire continent, but with various terminologies—"Estado of derecho" in Spanish, "Stato di dirito" in Italian, etc.

In modern times, the concept has been updated and the state of law has come to be identified with the liberal-democratic state. The Declaration of the Rights of the Man and of the Citizen (1789), taking John Locke's ideas of social philosophy as the true "bible of liberalism and individualism",

---

[9] Idem, p. 69.

[10] Albert Venn Dicey, *An Introduction to the Study of the Law of the Constitution*, LF ed., 1915, p. 44.

[11] "German authors are accustomed to acknowledging the German philosopher Immanuel Kant (1724–1804) at the forefront of their comments on the evolution of the rule of law. The rule of law was introduced with the sense of a 'constitutional state' by Kant, in later work after the American and French Constitutions had been adopted and towards the end of the eighteenth century. Kant's approach is based on the supremacy of the written constitution of a state", Geissler, Thorsten, The Konrad Adenauer Foundation, 2015, speech at the launch of the program "The values of the rule of law in the school curricula".

stated in art. 2 that "*The goal of any political association is the conservation of the natural and imprescriptible rights of man*" while art. 16 sharply asserts that "*Any society in which the guarantee of rights is not assured, nor the separation of powers determined, has no Constitution*".

The main principles of the rule of law are[12]:

- The state is based on the supremacy of the constitution and guarantees the security and constitutional rights of its citizens.
- Civil society is an equal partner with the state.
- State powers are separated into different compartments (legislative, executive and judicial) with separate and independent powers and responsibilities.
- Legislative power and democracy itself are related to the protection of these constitutional rights and principles.

It is therefore evident that the phrase "state of law" cannot be reduced to a simple logical concept. It gives expression to a fundamental constitutional need, according to which, as we mentioned earlier, the law is indispensable to the state and validates the purpose and effectiveness of the legal norms created; and the state is indispensable to the law to exercise and express power through the system of rules created.

Professor Tudor Drăganu, in "Introduction to the Theory and Practice of the State of Law", proposes an interesting and comprehensive definition of the concept of constitutional law: "*The state of law is considered such a State organized on the principle of the separation of state powers in the application of which justice acquires real independence and following through its legislation the promotion of the rights and freedoms inherent to human nature, ensures the strict observance of its regulations by the whole of its organs, in all their activity*".

The rule of law, which supposedly has its roots in antiquity, today defines "the supremacy of law" or, in legally specific terms, the preeminence of law. The preface to the European Convention on Human Rights and Fundamental Freedoms, states that "*the governments of European countries which are like-minded and have a common heritage of political traditions, ideals, freedom and the rule of law*". According to article 2 of the Treaty on European Union, the state of law is one of the fundamental values of the European Union. These regulations have come to emphasize that both the European Union as an institution itself, and

---

[12] Klaus Stern, *Das Staatsrecht der Bundesrepublik Deutschland,* I, 2nd edition, § 20, Munich 1984; Reinhold Zippelius, *Allgemeine Staatslehre/Politikwissenschaft*, 16th edition, §§ 8 II, 30-34, Munich 2010.

individual member states, have to adopt the concept of a "state of law", because it is one of the key political criteria that countries wishing to join the union must meet, including a system of laws (codes and other regulations) that are to be adopted under established procedures and not by discretionary decisions, thus guaranteeing the existence of functioning democracy and the respect of human rights, including the rights of persons belonging to minority groups.

The UN definition afforded to the "state of law" supports a similar ideology, stating that it is "*a principle of governance in which all persons, institutions and entities, public and private, including the State itself, are accountable to laws that are publicly promulgated, equally enforced and independently adjudicated, and which are consistent with international human rights norms and standards*"[13].

3. The state

Man, as a superior being, cannot live alone, in isolation, but must relate to his peers to evolve and survive. Humans are social by nature, each of us having primary instincts for forming communities, perhaps the oldest human need being the need to integrate into a society[14]. The dynamics of such a human need materialize in the interpersonal component and have led, throughout human evolution, to the formation of communities and been perfected in the establishment of rules of coexistence within them.

The evolution of the development of forms of social organization led to the emergence of a well-organized structural form of society, i.e. the emergence of the state.

The state, without benefiting from a well-defined definition, is therefore a superstructural institution. It is a primary instrument of political and administrative organization through which the functionality of the social system is exercised, relations between people, and the territory and population over which this organization exercises authority are regulated[15].

The totality of the legal rules and norms that regulate the conduct of people in social relations in a given community, which can be imposed by the coercive force of the state, represents **the legal system of the respective community.**

---

[13] United Nations, *Rule of Law*, online: https://www.un.org/ruleoflaw/what-is-the-rule-of-law/, consulted on 1.10.2019.

[14] The word "society" derives from the French word societé, with the Latin origin *societas*, meaning a friendly association with others and associate, comrade or business partner.

[15] https://dexonline.ro/definitie/stat, consulted on 12 September 2019.

4. The meanings of the notion of law

In the dictionary of the Romanian language, the word *drept* (law/right) has more than 138 paradigms, ranging from "*to get (or stay, take in) position perfectly vertical, standing still*" to the sense "*represent therefore, the shortest distance between two points, bluntly*" and "*corresponding to the right side of the body*" none of which validate the meaning of the term "right" in the phrase *stat de drept* (rule of law). In analyzing this term from a strictly juridical perspective, where the paradigm of the term of *drept* (law) has a broad meaning, this word points generically to a particular direction[16], related to the science concerned with the study of the norms of law, as summed up in the phrase "legal sciences".

The word *drept* (law) also references the "legal system" of a state, speaking of all legal norms developed or recognized by the state as aimed at organizing and ensuring discipline in the behaviour of its citizens within important social relationships, according to the social values of the respective society, and establishing rights and obligations whose compliance is ensured, if necessary, by the coercive power of the state. In the contemporary legal literature, law is defined as: "the *set of rules ensured and guaranteed by the state, which aim to organize and discipline human behavior in the main relations of society, in a specific climate of manifesting the coexistence of liberties, defending the essential rights of man and social justice*"[17].

In the present study, I primarily seek to emphasize the meaning that English gives to the word "law", especially in the phrase "rule of law", since a mere literary translation "of law" is not only insufficient, but also limited, in my opinion. This has not been very easy, since there have been multiple attempts to give a universally accepted definition of the word "law" in foreign legal doctrines. In fact, according to some theorists, such a definition cannot be given[18].

The English theorists McCoubrey and White[19], in trying to answer

---

[16] Voicu Costică, *Teoria Generală a Dreptului, Curs universitar*, Universul Juridic Publishing House, Bucharest, 2008, p. 7.

[17] Nicolae Popa, *Teoria generală a dreptului*, All Beck Publishing House, Bucharest, 1997, p. 97.

[18] Lord Lloyd of Hampstead, *Introduction to Jurisprudence*, third edition, Stevens & Sons, London, 1975, p. 39.

[19] Hilaire McCoubrey was a professor of law and director of postgraduate affairs at Hull University School of Law. He taught in areas such as legal theory, public international law, international law and armed conflict, and air and maritime law. Nigel D. White is Professor of Law in International Organizations at the University

the question "what is law", stated that the answer is one of the most difficult ones to give[20]. Glanville Williams[21] stated, more pragmatically, that the meaning of the word "law" depends on the context in which it is used[22]; Thurman Arnold[23] said that it is obviously impossible to define the word "law" and that it is equally obvious that the struggle to define this word will never be abandoned.

Although, in the foreign juridical literature, the meaning of "law" remains an intensely debated term, accepting the difficulty of limiting its meaning, we can observe that "law" primarily designates a system of rules, created and applied by social institutions or the government, to regulate the behavior of citizens in society—what we call "the system of law".

The Third New International Dictionary from Merriam-Webster[24] defines law as: "*a custom or a compulsory practice of a community; a rule or mode of conduct or action that is formally prescribed or recognized as mandatory by a controlling authority or is made compulsory by a sanction (as edict, decree, rescission, order, ordinance, statute, resolution, rule, judicial decision or use) applied, recognized or executed by the controlling authority*", equating to the "system of laws" in Romanian.

The Dictionary of the History of Ideas, published by Scribner in 1973, in the same way, defined the concept of "law" as being "*an explicit legal system, institutionalized and complex way of regulating human*

---

of Nottingham and teaches in the fields of jurisprudence and public international law.

[20] McCoubrey, Hilaire and White, Nigel D., *Textbook on Jurisprudence*, second edition, Blackstone Press Limited, 1996, p. 2.

[21] Glanville Llewelyn Williams, Welsh scholar, professor of law at the University of Cambridge and professor of jurisprudence at University College, London, was considered the most important scholar of criminal law in the United Kingdom.

[22] Williams Glanville (ed.), *International Law and the Controversy Concerning the Meaning of the Word "Law"*, revised version published in Laslett, "Philosophy, Politics and Society", 1956, p. 134.

[23] Thurman Wesley Arnold (June 2, 1891-November 7, 1969), a lawyer, social theorist and government official, an American and graduate of Princeton University in 1911 and a graduate of law at Harvard in 1914. In 1927, he was appointed dean of the Faculty of Law, the University of West Virginia, and taught at Yale Law School. His activities included the publication of two books—Symbols of Government (1935) and the Folklore of Capitalism (1937)—which enjoyed widespread national acclaim.

[24] Third New International Dictionary, Merriam-Webster, Inc., Springfield, Massachusetts.

behavior"[25].

The Oxford English Dictionary has, with direct reference to the "rule of law", defined the phrase as follows: "*The authority and influence of law in society, especially when seen as a constraint to individual and institutional behaviour; the principle that all members of companies (including those in the government) are also considered subject to publicly disclosed codes and legal processes*"[26], thus referring to the legal system of the state, which all citizens are subject to regardless of their social position.

5. Conclusions

In Romanian the phrase "state of law" is often used and it is obvious that it refers to a superstructural institution, a primary instrument of political and administrative organization, whose functioning is based on a system of laws that regulate relations between humans, with respect to four established principles: *the supremacy of the constitution and ensuring the safety and constitutional rights of citizens; civil society as an equal partner with the state; the separation of state powers and their division into different sections (legislative, executive and judiciary) with separate and independent powers and responsibilities; and where legislative power, as well as democracy itself, are linked to constitutional rights and principles.*

By the very use of this phrase, these principles have become misunderstood, adding a new paradigm to the word *drept* (law) in the dictionary of the Romanian language. But, by using the phrase "Romania is a state of law" followed by these principles, as detailed in other articles of fundamental law (the enumeration in the contents of art. 1 paragraph 3, respectively art. 16), this lexical construction can only be deemed a pleonasm.

Therefore, in conclusion, I hold that Romania is: a **democratic and social state**, whose system of laws ensures that "human dignity, the citizen's rights and freedoms, the free development of human personality, justice and political pluralism represent supreme values, in the spirit of the democratic traditions of the Romanian people and the ideals of the

---

[25] Philip P. Weiner (ed.), *Dictionary of the History of Ideas*, Charles Scribner's Sons, 1973.

[26] Oxford English Dictionary online (consulted on 13 September 2019). The term "rule of law" is sometimes used in other ways as well see Garner, Bryan A., *Black's Law Dictionary*, IX edition, Thomson Reuters, 2009, p. 1448. This source offers five definitions of the "rule of law": the main definition is "A legal principle of substance" and the second is "the supremacy of regulations through normative acts, as opposed to arbitrary power".

Revolution of December 1989", "law" being only a generic term for the notion of a "system of law", which is the basis of the functioning of the state as an institution.

Since a state institution cannot be democratic or social without a legal system based on these two principles, and the state as an institution cannot impinge on human dignity, the rights and freedoms of its citizens, the free development of human personality, and justice and political pluralism, these are all to be guaranteed on the sense of honour or arising from the conscience of society. I therefore suggest that the term "law", in the phrase "state of law", can only make a generic reference to the system of laws of the state, respecting the principles listed in the Romanian Constitution and the content of article 1 paragraph 3, as added to by article 16 on the "Equality of rights" (i.e. citizens are equal before the law and the authorities, without privilege or discrimination and that no one is above the law), thus sparing The Explanatory Dictionary of the Romanian Language the incorporation of a new paradigm of the word *drept* (law).

Bibliography

1. Albert Venn Dicey, *An Introduction to the Study of the Law of the Constitution*, LF ed., 1915.
2. Garner, Bryan A., *Black's Law Dictionary*, IX edition, Thomson Reuters, 2009.
3. Klaus Stern, *Das Staatsrecht der Bundesrepublik Deutschland,* I, 2nd edition, Munich, 1984.
4. Lord Lloyd of Hampstead, *Introduction to Jurisprudence*, third edition, Stevens & Sons, London, 1975.
5. Marius Andreescu, Claudia Andreescu, *Statul de drept. Semnificații constituționale și jurisprudențiale contemporane*, "Revista Universul Juridic", June 2019.
6. Mc Coubrey, Hilaire and White, Nigel D., *Textbook on Jurisprudence*, second edition, Blackstone Press Limited, 1996.
7. Muraru I, E. S. Tănăsescu, *Drept constituțional și instituții politice*, XIII edition, vol.1, C.H. Beck Publishing House, Bucharest, 2008.
8. Nicolae Popa, *Teoria generală a dreptului*, All Beck Publishing House, Bucharest, 1997.
9. Philip P. Weiner (ed.), *Dictionary of the History of Ideas*, Charles Scribner's Sons, 1973.
10. Reinhold Zippelius, *Allgemeine Staatslehre/Politikwissenschaft*, 16th edition, Munich, 2010.

11. Steluţa Ionescu, *Justiţia şi marile doctrine privind statul de drept*, "Studii de Drept Românesc", Year 20 (53), No. 1–2, 2008, p. 107–126.
12. Tamanaha, Brian Z., *As for the Rule of Law*, Cambridge University Press, 2004.
13. Voicu Costică, *Teoria Generală a Dreptului, Curs universitar*, Universul Juridic Publishing House, Bucharest, 2008.
14. Williams Glanville (ed.), *International Law and the Controversy Concerning the Meaning of the Word "Law"*, revised version published in Laslett, "Philosophy, Politics and Society", 1956.

SOCIAL ACTION IN THE PERSPECTIVE OF THE LAW-STATE RELATIONSHIP

PHD. STUDENT VASILE MILTIADE STANCIU[1]

Abstract: *We begin with the purpose of human activity and some of the realities both in Romania and elsewhere, which can be summarized in terms of: politics without healthy principles; market without morality; systemic pollution; science without humanism; inhuman inequalities; and legalism without soul etc. These all lead further and further away from the imperatives of human life in society, in terms of life, work and love. Using concepts that go beyond the field of law, such as social action, the author aims to find solutions derived from a holistic (systemic) vision in an economic interpretation, such as "integrated live integers". Thus, understanding the social action of the law, and especially understanding state social action, in terms of the demands of the "health of the live integer", can help identify some healthy solutions, beneficial for all parties and laying the foundation for an exchange of meaning in society. To that end, we believe that the implementation of these proposals can herald the beginning of a process of human and institutional re-spiritualization; something that is of great importance for the "Romania of Tomorrow".*

Keywords: *social action, the health of the live integer, the state loving people and truth, human and institutional respiritualization.*

***JEL Classification*:** K00, K10, K30

> *"A state wishing to be respected abroad and being strong and unshaken inside its borders has no other more precious treasure to preserve and cultivate than the feeling of national law. In the healthy and strong feeling of law in each individual, the state possesses the richest source of its power and the safest guarantee of its existence inside and outside the borders"*
> —Rudolf von Ihering

[1] Vasile Miltiade Stanciu, Bucharest University of Economic Studies, Romania: miltiade_stanciu@yahoo.com.

1. The concept of social action

All human beings systematically perform actions by which they pursue certain purposes, which are both acceptable and accepted by themselves and by the society where they're born, live, work, love and ultimately die. The individual uses specific means in order to achieve his/her purpose. As these actions take place in a certain social context generated by society, which influences and is influenced by the individual, they are essentially social actions.

In social action theory, we find: the author of the action, also referred to as the *agent*; the *purpose* of the social action; the *means* by which the agent realizes his/her purpose; the object of the human action, referred to as the *patient*; and the *product of the action*, as an object that he/she builds.

Human actions can be seen as "causal-productive relationships between the agent and the patient of the action"[2]. They are self-aware and generate goods and values, in terms of those products necessary for human accomplishment. It is obvious that if we compare the world of today with that of the past, we will find great differences and visible progress since then: from the behaviour of people who worshipped natural phenomena, considering those phenomena to have divine powers, and small, isolated localities that were vulnerable to predation; and from the total disregard of the rights of individuals to modern-day society, "in which, according to fixed laws, everyone must benefit from the heat of the sun of justice and equality, great progress has been made"[3]. All these advancements were possible only as a result of conscious, creative, and transformative human action. Of course, not all of these human actions took place simultaneously, but gradually, according to need, condition, and environment etc.

Contributions to the development of a philosophy and theory of action throughout known human history have appeared since ancient times in the work of several authors. Of these we may note the contribution of the Greek philosopher Aristotle who purportedly stated that "the basis of the state organization is the Constitution, which originates in the social nature of people"[4], of the theologians and philosophers of the Middle Ages such as Thomas Aquinas, and the "later philosophers of practice, Kant and Hegel",

---

[2] Tudosescu Ion, *Sistem social și acțiune umană. Expozeu de filosofie umană*, Fundația Romania de Mâine Publishing House Bucharest, 2008, p. 47.

[3] Ioan St. C., *Omul de doctrină și omul de acțiune*, Institutul de Arte Grafice "Eminescu", Bucharest, 1906, p. 3.

[4] Bădescu Mihai, *Socrate, Platon și Aristotel-promotori ai filosofiei dreptului în Grecia Antică*, "Pro Patria Lex", vol. 16, issue 1, 2016, pp. 17-31.

especially in terms of the *purpose-means* relationship within human action.

The German philosopher Friedrich Hegel raised the matter of the role of *means* in determining social life (seen as tools/instruments of work) and defining *purpose* as an activity that requires the use of tools, sometimes involving deceit and violence against society and nature.

The German philosopher, sociologist, and historian, Karl Marx, going further, tried to explain the dynamics of social life through the concept of *practice* and the implications of the *meaning of work* in the birth and development of human society.

After Marx, other philosophers continued to explain the concept of social actions. Thus, the Italian philosopher and politician Antonio Gramsci defined society as a system of social actions and referred to a *historical bloc*[5], while the Hungarian philosopher, aesthetician, literary historian, and critic, Georg Lukacs, placed the fundamental concept of work at the base of the social ontology.

The first half of the twentieth century saw the development of actionist thinking in what was termed *pragmatism*, having as its representatives the American scholars Charles Sanders Peirce (logician, mathematician and scientist), William James (a psychologist holding a degree in medicine who served as a professor at Harvard), and John Dewey (a philosopher, psychologist and educational reformer)[6].

To these authors, considered followers of the Marxist philosophy of praxis, other thinkers from the field of social and economic sciences can be added. These included the neo-Marxists of the Frankfurt School, with the prominent German scholars Max Horkheimer, the leader of The Frankfurt School and director of the Institute of Social Studies, who argued for humanity's desire to overcome personal suffering through social change[7], and Theodor Adorno, who advocated that action must come from consciousness[8]. To these we can further add the German-American philosopher, sociologist and political theoretician, Herbert Marcuse; the German philosopher and sociologist Jurgen Habermas; and the Canadian economist and diplomat John Kenneth Galbraith. The representatives of the Frankfurt School wanted, as part of a general plan, "to balance the State

---

[5] Boothman, Derek, *Gramsci's Historical Bloc: Structure, Hegemony and Dialectical Interactions*, "Movimento-revista de educação", Niterói, ano 4, n.6, pp. 131-150, Jan./Jun. 2017.

[6] https://www.iep.utm.edu/pragmati/#H1, accessed on 20.10.2019.

[7] Stanford Encyclopedia of Philosophy, *Max Horkheimer*, https://plato.stanford.edu/entries/horkheimer/, accessed on 20.10.2019.

[8] Encyclopedia of Philosophy, *Theodor Adorno*, https://www.iep.utm.edu/adorno/, accessed on 20.10.2019.

with the help of society and power with the help of law"[9].

Obviously, the problem of human (social) action has preoccupied sociology, and has been a subject of study of this scientific discipline and of others that derive from it. The study of human social action is probably very ancient, because, for example, in order for an individual or social group to avoid disrupting the positive activity of the community to which they belong through their actions, they must conform to the various norms, rules, general interests, and social values of that community. Moreover, this results in such social norms taking on a coercive role, obliging the individual to obey the demands of social life.

The German sociologist Max Weber studied the relationship between human action and social order, beginning with the fundamental features of action in his era and the methodological possibilities of the social sciences, utilizing the various methods and concepts, *means*, which he held distinct from those of the natural sciences.

The Italian sociologist and economist Vilfredo Pareto believed that the synthesis of human actions forms *social life*[10]. Analysing human actions, he concluded that there are two major categories of action: logical and non-logical. These include: non-experimental and logical actions; non-experimental and non-logical actions; experimental and logical actions; and experimental and non-logical actions. Pareto proposed that there is no connection between purpose and means, therefore non-logical actions are the foundation of social determinism, while logical actions have a limited role and the most important motivations of human actions are psychological ones related to human feelings.

Beginning with the definition of the global system of society, the American sociologist Talcott Parsons, in his social action analysis, focused on the existing interrelationships between the action systems made possible by an artificial language, namely that of science, taking a semiotic approach to human action.

The center of the action system structure conceived by Parsons is the correlation between the actions of individuals and their collective cooperation, and the cooperation of their action subsystems in the accomplishment of each stage or moment that forms general social action.

The *deontic logics* of the Finno-Swedish philosopher and Cambridge University professor, Georg Henrik von Wright, analysed human action through norms that generate rights and duties, specifically in disciplines of normative character (political and legal ethics etc.). He classified these

---

[9] Domenach, Jean-Marie, *Anchetă despre ideile contemporane*, French translation of Laura Mina, Humanitas Publishing House, Bucharest, 1991, p. 80.

[10] Pareto, Vilfredo, *Traité de sociologie générale*, Lausanne, Paris, 1917-1919.

norms (albeit, not very rigorously) into six categories, which he further divided into two[11]: the *major category*, including the rules of the game (assimilating also mathematical and logical aspects), the directives (the technical norms), and the prescriptions; and the *minor category*, divided into ideal rules, customs, and moral principles.

According to von Wright, *to act*, which does not have the same general explanation, is to deliberately *produce* or *prevent* a change in the world,˙ the consequence being that *refraining from action* leads to *not changing anything* or to *not letting anything happen*. Therefore, we have two types of action: a productive one and a preventive one, to which two types of refrainment correspond. More specifically, examples of actions are things such as: closing a window, opening a door, or signing an application etc.

A clear distinction is made between action and activity, the first one assuming a change and the second one a process. However, each change takes place through a process and the performance of an action involves an activity such as writing, translating, talking etc. In other words, the action and the activity are often complementary and the concept of *conduct* can be used to show both aspects. Obviously, there are rules on the prohibition of certain activities (no talking) or certain actions.

The Polish researcher, philosopher, and logician, Tadeusz Kotarbiński, analysed human action in terms of its efficiency, elaborating the theory of efficient action, known as *praxiology*, and integrating concepts of sociology, psycho-sociology, the efficient organization of work and production, and social philosophy etc.

In terms of efficient human action theory, Kotarbiński considered that it is: "the right place for introducing the distinction between the simple act, the multitude of acts, the composite act, the positive cooperation, the negative cooperation (fight or conflict), the assistance relationship, the obstruction, the facilitation, the generation of difficulties, the preparation, the planning, the execution, the control, the command and leadership, organization, etc."[12].

Furthermore, "the root cause of social actions is external to the subject, being, first of all, economic"[13], even if the impulse towards action is born within him/her, in his/her psyche. And in order for the individual not

---

[11] Von Wright Georg Henrick, *Norm and Action: A Logical Enquiry*, Routledge and Kegan Paul, London 1963.

[12] Kotarbinski, Tadeusz, *Praxiological Propositions and their Proof*, in Logic, Methodology and Philosophy of Science, Stanford University, 1962, p. 228.

[13] Muraru, Ion, *Acțiune socială și comportamentul individual*, Politică Publishing House, Bucharest, 1986, p. 37.

to affect any of his/her peers through his/her actions, a norm must be established to regulate any of his/her antisocial attitudes.

In this context, we agree with the statement made about a hundred years ago by Mircea Georgescu, a doctor of laws, who stated that "the law does not tend to suppress the internal predispositions or tendencies for injustice [of individuals]; it concerns only the *act that occurred* in connection to the birth of any infringement of other people's rights"[14].

Therefore, the social need to ensure order and a good standard of coexistence among individuals, and to create the necessary framework for the smooth running of happenings within society is imposed through certain behavioural rules in society, "without which coexistence would have been impossible"[15].

In the same spirit, the Romanian researcher Professor Ion Craiovan, notes that: "no form of human association can function properly without establishing a minimum of rules of conduct, concluding that society is born at the same time with the genesis of the norm"[16].

Basically, people accomplish things exclusively by their "transformative action upon their own extant environment, which ends with the production (or facilitation of production) of goods and values necessary for their material and spiritual living"[17]; these are not offered to them by the natural environment, but must be produced by people.

Through creative human participation in the production/transformation objectified in work, people become successful on multiple planes. Being in relationships with other people (maintaining rapport) and in order to live together, it is necessary to establish certain conducts that are accepted by society in different areas of social life that it regulates, in political, familial, and economic terms etc.

2. The social action of law

People cannot be separated from the community in which they live, work, and love, and considering that the meaning of the human need for social belonging can be expressed by the phrase "people, as social beings,

---

[14] Georgescu, Mircea, *Criteriul biologic în Drept*, Imprimeria Fondul Cărților Funduare, Cluj, 1932, p. 31.

[15] Paraschiv, Elena, *Izvoarele formale ale dreptului,* C. H. Beck Publishing House, Bucharest, 2007, p. 1.

[16] Craiovan, Ion, *Filosofia dreptului sau dreptul ca filosofie*, 2nd ed., ProUniversitaria Publishing House, Bucharest, 2019, p. 33.

[17] Tudosescu, Ion, *Acțiune umană și existență*, Fundația România de Mâine Publishing House, Bucharest, 2018, p. 61.

feel the need to live in a community"[18], it is natural for human beings to enter into different social relationships with their peers. These relationships can be "political, economic, cultural, familial etc."[19] and take place within human society, about which the Romanian sociologist Dimitrie Gusti noted: "it is in fact the synthetic totality of those four manifestations, of the economic, spiritual, legal and political manifestations"[20].

The German sociologist, philosopher and essayist Georg Simmel emphasized that: "a society exists where more individuals enter into interaction relationships (...) due to certain instincts or to the desire to achieve certain goals"[21].

However, these rapports in interaction, as Simmel called them, based on the continuous and mutual influence of human beings, take place in pre-established settings where they socialize (society) and in which some rules, prescriptions, and obligations etc. must be established. As such, each individual must observe these in order to maintain social order and "contribute to establishing a relative state of balance and harmony, but never definitive"[22], because of the impact of disturbing actions, events, phenomena, and social relations etc.

Therefore, human action, understood as deliberately producing or preventing change in the outside world, implies that human beings refrain from taking an action whose possible consequence is the leaving of something unchanged or letting something happen[23].

The rules that organize human action, in other words the regulation of the rational mode of living in social life, are established through social norms. Basically, the norms provide people with the opportunity to anticipate the actions of others and to prepare appropriate responses, in line with the culture of the respective community, thus being a kind of "guide to

---

[18] Niemesch, Mihail, *Reglementările sociale între tabuuri antice și internet ca factor de configurare a dreptului* in "Impactul transformărilor socio-economice și tehnologice la nivel național, european și mondial", vol.6, no.6, 2015, pp. 68-72.

[19] Penculescu, Gheorghe, *Principii de drept*, Științifica Publishing House, Bucharest, 1958, p. 9.

[20] Gusti, Dimitrie, *Cunoaștere și acțiune în serviciul națiunii,* vol. II, Cartea Echipelor, Fundația Culturală Regală "Principele Carol", Bucharest, 1946, p. 18.

[21] Simmel, Georg, *Sociologie. Studii privind formele socializării*, German translation: Ion Nastasia and Maria Nastasia, Sigma IG, Publishing House, Chișinău, 2000, p. 12.

[22] Craiovan, Ion, *op. cit.*, 2019, p. 34.

[23] Von Wright, Georg Henrik, *Logica deontică și teoria generală a acțiunii* in *Norme, valori, acțiune. Analiza logică a discursului practic, cu aplicații în etică și în drept*, Text selection, translation and introductory study: Sorin Vieru, Dragan Stoianovici, Politică Publishing House, Bucharest, 1979, pp. 140-141.

the behaviour of each individual and reducing the ambiguity that most individuals consider intolerable"[24]. In other words, through thesew norms, society becomes a "cosmos" organized in a hierarchy of imperative, prescriptive, and sanctioning order of conduct[25].

Within the wider framework of social norms that can be classified according to different criteria, such as incorporated values, the field of activity, the mode of manifestation, their degree of generality, and their content etc., the legal norms or norms of law can be found.

From the multitude of definitions of a legal norm, we may keep in mind in our research, that of the Romanian professor Nicolae Popa, for whom such a norm is: "a general and compulsory rule of conduct, whose purpose is to ensure the social order, a rule that can be enforced using state levers, even by constraint if needed"[26].

The social relationships between people who are regulated by legal norms form legal relationships, implying that the latter are established by legal norms, created by the state, and guaranteed by the constraining force of the state. As such, we can talk about different historical moments when both the state and the law coincided[27].

Of course, the legal norms and, in particular the law, undergo organic development, in close connection with the development of the society of which they are a part: "all those legal norms that settled down slowly by the autonomous conclusion of the business of law, through relationships among people and also all those abstractions, conclusions and rules that science deduces analytically from existing law and to whom it offers consciousness"[28].

The Romanian sociologist, Anton Golopenția, stated that: "the law measures reality according to a certain norm of the constitution imposed or taken over in that state by the dominant power and of a legal system

---

[24] Boncu Ștefan, Curelaru Mihai, Nastas Dorin, Onici Octavian, *Norme, legi și avertizori* in "Psihologia socială" no. 40 (II), 2017, pp. 69-82, p. 70.

[25] Craiovan, Ion, *Doctrina juridică*, ALL Beck Publishing House, Bucharest, 1999, p. 26.

[26] Popa, Nicolae, *Teoria generală a dreptului*, 5th ed. C. H. Beck Publishing House, Bucharest, 2014, p. 129.

[27] In this regard see: Ceterchi, Ioan et al., *Teoria generală a statului și dreptului*, Didactică și Pedagogică Publishing House, Bucharest, 1967; Hanga, Vladimir, *Crestomație pentru studiul istoriei statului și dreptului R.P.R.*, vol I, State Publishing House for Economic and Legal Literature, Bucharest, 1955; Hanga Vladimir, Pascu Ștefan, *Crestomație pentru studiul istoriei statului și dreptului R.P.R.*, vol II, Științifică Publishing House, Bucharest, 1958.

[28] Von Ihering, Rudolf, *Lupta pentru drept*, traducere din limba germană de Sandi Constantinescu, Institutul de Arte Grafice "Modernă", Constanța, 1872, p. 8.

corresponding to this constitution"[29]. This is what Aristotle also expressed when he stated "law is the order of the political community", meaning that no political community can function properly outside the law.

The Romanian professor, Mihai Bădescu, asserts that: "law, far from being the product of special and exceptional causes, is a necessary product of human nature, it is a common phenomenon, in every era, for all peoples and human individuals (...) has the role of promoting and defending the *main social value*"[30].

The Romanian scientist, Dimitrie Gusti, noted: "law is nothing more than an aspect of social life (as the etymology shows us: *dirigere, Recht, dirito, droit*, means direction and the Latin *jus* comes from Sanskrit *ju*, which means to bind). Law is the principle of direction, of social cohesion; it gives to the company the character of definition and consistency; therefore the science of law is a social science, and not a purely technical one"[31].

In other words, order within a society or community etc. is given by law, which is practically its product at the same time. In practice, social life, in all its aspects, is governed and regulated by laws and a formal legal character.

Therefore, *a first consequence (action) of the law is the observance of the existing rules*, no matter what they are, *by any of the citizens upon whom those rules have an impact*, which also implies that the observance of the rules corresponds to an awareness that they must be observed. In other words, *law is an adaptation to a dynamic concrete reality.*

In this context, considering the appreciation of the "spiritual man", the characterization of law by the Romanian researcher and professor Ion Craiovan is not only current and topical, but of great openness as well. He states that: "law, though created, creates its creators; it is closed (through juridicity), but also open (to given elements and other subsystems); autonomous (self-regulating), but also constrained (from outside it); organized and organizing; coherent (*hic et nunc*) and contradictory (among subsystems); homogeneous (by its specificity) and discontinuous (porous, permeable); informed, but also informative; material and ideal (valuable)

---

[29] Golopenția, Anton, *Opere complete. Vol I. Sociologie,* Enciclopedică Publishing House, Bucharest, 2002, p. 27.

[30] Bădescu, Mihai, *Filosofia dreptului în România interbelică,* Sitech Publishing House, Craiova, 2018, pp. 24-25.

[31] Gusti, Dimitrie, *Sociologie juridică. Culegere de texte*, Introductory study, selection and systematization of texts by Ion Vlăduț, Didactică și Pedagogică R. A Publishing House, Bucharest, 1997, p. 36.

and so on"[32].

The law has been configured by several important factors, which can be grouped into three distinct but interdependent categories: *the natural environment*; *the social-political environment*; and *the human environment.* These must be in permanent harmony, the law having the task of establishing the correspondence of legal norms created with and for each of them separately and with the whole formed by them as well. Therefore, the law, in terms of its content (expressed as all interdependent elements, sides, and connections that express the will and social interests that must be formulated and guaranteed by the state through its bodies) is in a state of "permanent change"[33]. This determines the essence of legal reality, which constantly rebuilds itself, through an evolutionary process and depending on the needs of society.

Secondly, we witness, in this way, *the social action of the law upon the human being and, as well, upon the human collective of which he/she is part.* This social action involves two types of action: direct actions and mediating actions, between which there are mutual inter-conditioning relationships.

For example, direct training and educational-social action, including didactic and educational activity, as well as cultural and formative-axiological activity, is conditioned by mediating social actions such as the elaboration and improvement of legal norms in the field, corroborated by legal actions regulating human rights and freedoms etc.

Therefore, *the social action of the law also targets the individual, as a unique social being, through regulations concerning his/her rights and duties, as well as the society of which he/she is a part*, as a whole.

As for the actions performed by each individual, in order to achieve the proposed goals by particular means, the law, understood as all legal regulations existing in public circulation with immediate or future applicability, designed, legislated, and enforced by institutions having a role expressly established for that end, aims to regulate the field of social life.

Therefore, in law, the actual author of an action, *the agent*, is the institution that develops the complex of normative documents; *the purpose* is the regulation of conduct in the field of legislation; *the means* is made up of the normative documents themselves; *the patient* is the regulated social field; and the *product of the action* is given by the reality that constructs it by applying the normative documents.

---

[32] Craiovan, Ion, *Despre triada metodă-știință-drept*, "Revista Univers Strategic", 2018, Issue 35, pp. 154-162, p. 158.

[33] See in this regard Djuvara Mircea, *Teoria generală a dreptului*. Vol I, Socec Publishing House, Bucharest 1930, p. 16.

In other words, "through its normative function, the law is constituted as a factor for programming the individual's freedom of action"[34], but being closely linked to the social, economic and political realities of the state.

In fact, *through the action of law expressed by norms that the human individual must adhere to in order to regulate his/her own behaviour in society, he/she meets and (sometimes) exceeds his/her own existential condition.*

3. The social action of the state

Taking into account the aspects presented above, we believe that the law is created by the life of a society itself and for this reason, phrases such as "the law is alive in its destinies"[35]; "life creates the law"[36]; "cause or effect, law coexists with social phenomena and thus the history of law can be considered as the history of social phenomena"[37]; the history of law is part of national history"[38]; "law is a consequence, a product of human coexistence in society form"[39], etc. reflect the process of creation and the historical evolution of the law, which is closely linked to the evolution of the state.

To that end, the historical process includes the genesis of law, along with the intensification of social relationships, the creation and multiplication of production factors, and the increase of the degree of human interaction etc. materialized, for example, in the social division of labour, the division of society into rich and poor, with the polarization of wealth, usually to only one social class, regardless of the historical time period, the occurrence of the institution of marriage, and the occurrence and strengthening of the state, etc.

---

[34] Albici, Mihail, *Realitatea socială a dreptului,* Hamangiu Publishing House, Bucharest 2017, p. 36.

[35] Manolescu, M. I., *Știința dreptului și artele juridice*, Continent XXI Publishing House, Bucharest, 1993, p. 34.

[36] Fotino, George, *Curs de istoria dreptului românesc I. 1940-1941,* Bucharest University, Law Faculty 1940, p. 8.

[37] Peretz, Ioan, *Curs de istoria dreptului român. Partea I. Originile dreptului român,* Tip. Ziarului "Curierului Judiciar" Publishing House, Bucharest, 1915, pp. 3-4.

[38] Onișor, Victor, *Istoria dreptului român. pentru anul I. al facultății de drept (curs de licență)*, Tipografia "Libertatea", Orăștie, Cluj, 1921, pp. 3-4.

[39] Bălănescu Rosetti Ion, *Dreptul în general și noțiunile sale fundamentale. Expunere introductivă la studiul dreptului,* Ziarul "Universul" Publishing House, Bucharest, 1937, p. 12.

The moment when law occurred is the subject of different and diverse points of view[40], not being clarified by the theoreticians of the field, therefore, the establishment of the law as a full entity can be associated with the establishment of public power as state power. In fact, the state and the law are in a relationship of interdependence, as proposed by the Austrian jurist and philosopher Hans Kelsen.

There is a relation between law and state, as acknowledged by many theorists, "the state having the task not only to impose justice, but also having the means to do justice, which is to use violence in order to prevent and punish violations of justice"[41]. There have been opinions for and against the state from this perspective, especially of the monopoly exercised by the state, but, assuming as a hypothesis the *achievement of the public good*, the social action of the state must be analysed and corrected whenever necessary using the mechanisms available within the democracies that exist today, both in Romania and elsewhere.

However, we adopt the idea that "the state is the main institution of society (...) being the instrument of social leadership"[42]. And we also note that, at present, there is no other institution created by the people for the people to pursue the good of all the people, because the law can only be achieved by the state, as the "rule of law is nothing else but a ceaseless fight against illegality that attacks that rule of law"[43].

Dimitrie Gusti said that: "the state as a regulatory and organizing category of the nation, in the form of the national state, must create an order according to the social units that make up the nation"[44].

We believe that the state is the mirror of its citizens and the question asked by von Ihering more than a hundred years ago is still valid today: "If a man is not taught to bravely defend his own rights, how could

[40] See in this regard Duverger, Maurice, *Institutions politiquees et droit constitutionnel*, P.U.F, Paris, 1956; Popescu, Sofia, *Concepții contemporane despre drept*, Academiei Române Publishing House, Bucharest, 1985; Popa, Nicolae, *Teoria generală a dreptului*, Actami Publishing House, Bucharest, 1996; Craiovan, Ion, *Tratat de teoria generală a dreptului*, 3rd ed., Universul Juridic Publishing House, Bucharest, 2015.

[41] Craiovan, Ion, *op. cit.*, 2019, p. 412.

[42] Capcelea, Valeriu, *Filosofia juridică. Introducere în istoria filosofiei juridice și în studiul principalelor domenii ale ei*, Universul Juridic Publishing House, Bucharest, 2019, p. 254.

[43] Chevallier, Jacques, *Statul de drept*, French translation of Diana Dănișor, Universitaria Publishing House, Craiova, 2012, p. 148.

[44] Gusti, Dimitrie, *Considerații asupra unui sistem de sociologie, etică și politică* in *Opere,* vol I, Academia Republicii Socialiste România Publishing House, Bucharest, 1968, pp. 367-368.

he still feel the urge to willingly risk his life and wealth for the law of society?"

We debate the transition from the *rule of law* to the *state loving people and truth*, combating, through faith-based policies, the structural causes of poverty and inequality that destroy human dignity and create pollution, which destroys the balance of the "common live integer", and human and institutional corruption that manifests itself as a "social cancer", within an anthropological view. We support, in terms of conscience, the primacy of the human being through free, creative, participatory and community-based work for the common good, as John Kenneth Galbraith called it in *The Good Society—in focus: the good for the people*![45]

As Pope Francis said, "the state must assume the role of encouraging, integrating, empowering, delegating, but without giving up its original mission: to take care of the common good of the people"[46].

We hold the hypothesis that, from the creation of the conditions **that determined the occurrence of the state**, although the genetic endowment of different people is different, being thin or fat, tall or short, with genetic predispositions to become rich or not, they are at the same time complementary, forming a WHOLE.

Throughout history, due to this different human genetic endowment, the possibility of some people having more and others less has been constantly emphasized over time. Not only is there a detachment from the collective by some people who accumulated more than others, giving birth to the idea of private property, the increase in difference between people on account of accumulation, in conjunction with unequal growth of its development and implicit benefits, *led to the occurrence of the state*, but also to the *lack of an adequate reaction of human communities to these social inequities*. This has all determined **the necessity for creating better and more suitable forms and systems of organization to solve these discrepancies.**

Therefore, ***the state is a historical phenomenon*, which did not exist in the beginning and *only occurred once conditions for it to form and develop existed.***

As such, *the state has come to govern the social relations among individuals, individual-groups, and groups having different interests* (contradicting one another), using its force to constrain and against those who oppose it. Therefore, *the state will not disappear in any future higher*

---

[45] Galbraith, John Kenneth, *Societatea perfectă. La ordinea zilei: binele omului*, Eurosong&Book Publishing House, Bucharest, 1997.

[46] Papa Francisc, *Adevărata putere este slujirea*, translation Geaniana Tivdă, Oana Gabor, Pauline Publishing House, Bucharest, 2014, p. 176.

order, even if it is diminished and the conditions that determined its emergence no longer exist; but it will still be necessary (possibly with diminished functions), considering that the genetic endowment of humanity has not changed, and so exceptions appear.

We believe that human societies, here and elsewhere, need a *strong, independent and sovereign state*; a natural and normal *legal framework* that helps and does not raise problems in and of interpretation; *honest people* to be promoted to and working in appropriate positions; and *a culture that forms young individuals who are respectful towards their country*. People who have grown up with values such as honesty, truth, justice etc., from which some of our fellows have distanced themselves since 1989, so that **the world of tomorrow can be the deliberate, planned, conscious and responsible result of all the individuals of today created for the individuals of tomorrow, based on the experience gained and not only to serve those of today!**

To this end, **we propose a set of measures**[47] **for Romania**, which, in our opinion, requires **a rethinking of the place and the role that the state must hold**. More than that, it requires a rethinking of the role of the social action of the state in order to put the development of our country on a new basis, in relation to long-standing Romanian traditions and values, as well as taking into account the perspectives of contemporary science and information society.

We need to draw up short, medium and long term development plans, so that Romania can reach at least the level of 1989, which can be considered a landmark in terms of the level obtained and which has not been achieved since, with the goal of reaching the developmental level of the most advanced states. To achieve these objectives we must focus on the following:

Increasing domestic capital, so that we no longer depend on foreign investors. Obviously, we do not deny the importance of foreign direct investment (FDI), but our economic foundation must be formed by indigenous capitalists so as not to rely on unfavourable international conjunctions and on certain group interests that contradict national ones.

The establishment of high productivity agricultural units. Developing systems for the sale of agricultural products, so that agricultural producers can be relieved of this task. This can materialize only with state support.

---

[47] These proposals have been published in Stanciu Vasile Miltiade, *Statul în timpul și după Cantemir*, pp. 370-388 in Dogaru Mircea, Ciobanu Viorel, Dimitrie, *Cantemir și conștiința unității românilor. Studii și articole dedicate Centenarului Marii Uniri*, Universul Academic Publishing House, Bucharest, 2018.

Diversification of production. The state must remain the main coordinator, which has remained fundamental, as was highlighted by the state's involvement in the latest global crisis in order to make it come to an end. Relying on private enterprise, it is impossible to achieve economic, political, and military independence, even with local capital.

The involvement of the state (through effective control) of prices, even under free market conditions, considering the cost price and the market price (demand-supply), even if it is artificial. High demand causes prices to be maintained at an advantageous level for both buyer and seller; however, it is not desirable that some people become rich and others poor.

Concrete economic measures in order to limit poverty. Monetary profit should not be the goal itself, but it must be quantified for other purposes as well. It is good to borrow models from other countries as well, but only those that can be sustainably assimilated by our citizens and institutions. Copying solutions completely from other countries and translating them into local public policies has not been beneficial for our country and will never be so.

The state must not alienate national wealth (from the land of our home country), which is a good that belongs to all citizens of the state, as expressly stipulated in the Romanian Constitution, Article 1 paragraph 1, which provides that *Romania is a national state, sovereign and independent, unitary and indivisible*, and Article 3 paragraph 1, which states that *the territory of Romania is inalienable*. These are constitutional provisions that, if not observed, will implicitly lead to the *diminution of the territory of the state, of its sovereignty, and of its independence.*

Taking measures to reduce phenomena such as labour migration (making investments, either directly by the state from its budget, or by individuals, as the case may be), causing a drastic decrease in the country's population (payment of an allowance for all mothers, regardless of the salary before birth, calculated at the level of the highest salary paid to such mothers), and greater stimulation of certain professions (doctors, largely accomplished at present; teachers; those who work in difficult conditions), so as to ensure a consistent balance for them.

Finding solutions for choosing leaders, so that they are not tied to individual or group interests, expressly observing Article 16 paragraph 1 of the Constitution of Romania, which states that *citizens are equal before the law and before public authorities, with no privileges and with no discrimination*. We consider that *the best choice of the leaders of state institutions at all levels must be made through competition*, with regard to scientific background and moral and scientific behaviour, so as to enjoy the respect and esteem of the collective from which he/she originates etc., even if this implies the adoption of a special organic law.

For this, it is necessary ***to create specific institutions for the training of management personnel at all levels***, so that only people with the highest training are chosen to compete for various positions. For example, the president of the country, the prime minister, and the ministers should all hold doctorates in administrative and/or legal sciences, as the case may be.

Training for the future occupation of management positions must take place in advance, at least ten years before applying the procedure for taking up a public position through competition.

Persons selected for public functions must be independent, not involved in economic activities, not be part of political parties, not be under criminal investigation, and have a high moral profile. They must fight in defence of the country, in accordance with articles 54 and 55 of the Constitution of Romania, which state that: *loyalty to the country is a sacred duty* (paragraph 1) and *citizens entrusted with public functions and military men are responsible for faithfully fulfilling their duties and, for this purpose, will take the oath required by law* (paragraph 2). Also, *citizens have the right and obligation to defend Romania* (paragraph 1), even if a draft *de lege ferenda* is required for a change in this regard.

Establishing taxes and fees corresponding to income, differentiated according to its size.

Pensions should be calculated fairly, so that there is a fair ratio between the highest and the lowest pension, because the needs of retired people are generally similar and there is no justification for a category of retired people to have an extremely high pension compared to others (the smallest pension should be sufficient to cover the general needs of life).

The gradual replacement of the current political class through participatory democracy that gives the right of every citizen to occupy any public position, by contest, fulfilling the conditions provided for in its respective function, including Parliament.

Reducing the central and local administrative apparatus, by making it more efficient.

At the same time, the ***state must be receptive to all tendencies that contradict creation***, and not legislate the "rights of individuals", even if the international institutions of which Romania is a member also intervene. An example of this is homosexuality and marriage between two persons of the same gender.

Observing the important role of education in the development of the state, a ***unique legislative framework for the evolution of Romania's education and development must be prepared*** (as strategic plans), in the short, medium, and long term (a few decades), so that frequent political changes do not disturb strong public policy any longer.

This framework must correlate to the strategies developed up to the present day and completed by elements for observing the "health of the live integer" paradigm, which traces the total evolution of an individual from birth up to postgraduate training, including continuous training (in various forms and of short duration) and must align consistently to the development strategies of Romania. It is fundamental that these documents, once adopted, are translated into practice, regardless of the "colour" of the governing party/coalition. Otherwise, we are talking only about forms without funding or about assigning resources without having the desired achievement. In order to fulfil this goal, it is necessary to have sanctions for those that do not translate legislative provisions into practice and these must be applied as soon as a deficiency is discovered.

4. For reflection and action

Beyond the concepts of the *social action of the law* or the *social action of the state*, we raise the issue of responsibly using scientific knowledge—at present humanity has access to knowledge that could not have been imagined even a few centuries ago. The issue is not one of knowledge itself, but whom it serves, how it is used, and how it will be used both today and in the future.

Any activity of social life that does not endanger individual and family health, the health of human communities and regional and state institutions, as well as the health of the environment, generates *win-win* situations for all participants. It does not generate gain for some of them and loss for others, as it has until now in many of the contexts that exist both in Romania and elsewhere. In fact, the *win-win principle* is also the essence of wisdom in terms of the responsible use of knowledge for the "the health of the live integer".

The serious problems faced by a large part of our world, such as endemic poverty; politics without sound principles; free markets without morality; systemic pollution; science without humanism; legalism without soul; the arms race and terrorism etc. have not been solved and in many cases have developed and worsened, becoming serious problems born of our disproportionate evolution, as noted by Pope John Paul II[48].

[48] Papa Ioan Paul al II-lea., *Enciclice*, ARCB Publishing House, Bucharest, 2008, p. 32.

What does this mean? In fact, we have not solved the root causes of these problems and we have not tried to reinvent or to spiritualize the ways people live. The issue we are raising concerns "changing our minds" and moving towards another way of thinking and living that originates in the belief that prosperity and poverty are in us as human beings, in us as families, in us as business organizations, and in us as a nation and as a people, and not outside ourselves[49].

To these social realities, like many other current and foreseeable challenges, the action of the law and the action of the state, in particular, must respond.

Finally, we consider that it is necessary, starting from current realities, for each of us to engage in introspection and answer at least one fundamental question: *what should I do so that, in the future, I can live better on this earth, in my country, together with my peers?*

In conclusion, the permanent rethinking of the state's role and functions, as well as of the social action of the state, is an important and dynamic problem and one which must be of concern to a wide range of specialists in many fields, who should constitute the membership of trans-disciplinary research groups.

But let us not forget that all such solutions must be developed by patriotic, visionary, and honest people, who love their country and really believe that TOMORROW is always built TODAY and based on the lessons learned YESTERDAY!

Bibliography

1. Albici, Mihail, *Realitatea socială a dreptului,* Hamangiu Publishing House, Bucharest, 2017.
2. Bădescu, Mihai, *Filosofia dreptului în România interbelică,* Sitech Publishing House, Craiova, 2018.
3. Bădescu, Mihai, *Socrate, Platon și Aristotel-promotori ai filosofiei dreptului în Grecia Antică*, "Pro Patria Lex", vol. 16 Issue 1, 2016, pp. 17-31.
4. Bălănescu, Rosetti Ion, *Dreptul în general și noțiunile sale fundamentale. Expunere introductivă la studiul dreptului,* Ziarul "Universul" Publishing House, Bucharest, 1937.
5. Boncu Ștefan, Curelaru Mihai, Nastas Dorin, Onici Octavian, *Norme, legi și avertizori*, "Psihologia socială" no. 40 (II), 2017, pp.

[49] Costea Carmen, Popescu Constantin, Taşnadi Alexandru (coord.), *Criza e în Noi*, ASE Publishing House, Bucharest, 2011, pp. 451-470.

69-82.
6. Capcelea, Valeriu, *Filosofia juridică. Introducere în istoria filosofiei juridice și în studiul principalelor domenii ale ei*, Universul Juridic Publishing House, Bucharest, 2019.
7. Ceterchi, Ioan et al., *Teoria generală a statului și dreptului*, Didactică și Pedagogică Publishing House, Bucharest, 1967.
8. Chevallier Jacques, *Statul de drept*, French translation by Diana Dănișor, Universitaria, Publishing House, Craiova, 2012.
9. Costea Carmen, Popescu Constantin, Taşnadi Alexandru (coord.), *Criza e în Noi*, ASE Publishing House, Bucharest, 2011.
10. Craiovan, Ion, *Despre triada metodă-știință-drept*, "Revista Univers Strategic", 2018, Issue 35, pp. 154-162.
11. Craiovan, Ion, *Doctrina juridică*, ALL BECK Publishing House, Bucharest, 1999.
12. Craiovan, Ion, *Filosofia dreptului sau dreptul ca filosofie*, 2nd ed., Pro Universitaria Publishing House, Bucharest, 2019.
13. Craiovan, Ion, *Tratat de teoria generală a dreptului*, 3rd ed., Universul Juridic Publishing House, Bucharest, 2015.
14. Djuvara, Mircea, *Teoria generală a dreptului*. Vol. I, Socec Publishing House, Bucharest, 1930.
15. Domenach, Jean-Marie, *Anchetă despre ideile contemporane*, French translation by Laura Mina, Humanitas Publishing House, Bucharest, 1991.
16. Duverger Maurice, *Institutions politiquees et droit constitutionnel*, P.U.F, Paris, 1956.
17. Fotino George, *Curs de istoria dreptului românesc I. 1940-1941*, Bucharest University, Law Faculty, 1940.
18. Galbraith John Kenneth, *Societatea perfectă. La ordinea zilei: binele omului*, Eurosong & Book, Publishing House, Bucharest, 1997.
19. Georgescu, Mircea, *Criteriul biologic în Drept*, Imprimeria Fondul Cărților Funduare, Cluj, 1932.
20. Golopenția, Anton, *Opere complete. Vol I. Sociologie,* Enciclopedica Publishing House, Bucharest, 2002.
21. Gusti, Dimitrie, *Considerații asupra unui sistem de sociologie, etică și politică* în *Opere*, vol. I, Academia Republicii Socialiste România Publishing House, Bucharest, 1968.
22. Gusti, Dimitrie, *Cunoaștere și acțiune în serviciul națiunii. Volumul II*, Cartea Echipelor, Fundația Culturală Regală "Principele Carol", Bucharest, 1946.
23. Gusti, Dimitrie, *Sociologie juridică. Culegere de texte*, Introductory study, selection and systematization of texts by Ion Vlăduț, Didactică

și Pedagogică R. A. Publishing House, Bucharest, 1997.
24. Hanga, Vladimir, *Crestomație pentru studiul istoriei statului și dreptului R.P.R.*, vol. I, State Publishing House for Economic and Legal Literature, Bucharest, 1955.
25. Hanga, Vladimir, Pascu Ștefan, *Crestomație pentru studiul istoriei statului și dreptului R.P.R.*, vol. II, Științifica Publishing House, Bucharest, 1958.
26. Von Ihering, Rudolf, *Lupta pentru drept*, German translation by Sandi Constantinescu, Institutul de Arte Grafice "Modernă", Constanța, 1872.
27. Ioan, St. C., *Omul de doctrină și omul de acțiune*, Institutul de Arte Grafice "Eminescu", Bucharest, 1906.
28. Manolescu, M. I., *Știința dreptului și artele juridice*, Continent XXI Publishing House, Bucharest, 1993.
29. Muraru, Ion, *Acțiune socială și comportamentul individual*, Politică Publishing House, Bucharest, 1986.
30. Niemesch, Mihail, *Reglementările sociale între tabuuri antice și internet ca factor de configurare a dreptului,* "Impactul transformărilor socio-economice și tehnologice la nivel național, european și mondial", vol. 6, no. 6, 2015, pp. 68-72.
31. Onișor, Victor, *Istoria dreptului român. pentru anul I al facultății de drept (curs de licență)*, Tipografia "Libertatea", Orăștie, Cluj, 1921.
32. Papa Francisc, *Adevărata putere este slujirea*, translation Geaniana Tivdă, Oana Gabor, Pauline Publishing House, Bucharest, 2014.
33. Papa Ioan Paul al II-lea, *Enciclice*, ARCB Publishing House, Bucharest, 2008.
34. Paraschiv, Elena, *Izvoarele formale ale dreptului,* C.H. Beck Publishing House, Bucharest, 2007.
35. Pareto, Vilfredo, *Traité de sociologie générale*, Lausanne, Paris, 1917-1919.
36. Penculescu, Gheorghe, *Principii de drept*, Științifică Publishing House, Bucharest, 1958.
37. Peretz, Ioan, *Curs de istoria dreptului român. Partea I. Originile dreptului român*, Tip. Ziarului "Curierului Judiciar" Publishing House, Calea Rahovei 5, Bucharest 1915.
38. Popa, Nicolae, *Teoria generală a dreptului*, 5th ed., C. H. Beck Publishing House, Bucharest, 2014.
39. Popescu, Sofia, *Concepții contemporane despre drept*, Academia Romȃna Publishing House, Bucharest 1985.
40. Simmel, Georg, *Sociologie. Studii privind formele socializării*, German translation of Ion Nastasia and Maria Nastasia, Sigma IG

Publishing House, Chisinau, 2000.
41. Stanciu, Vasile Miltiade, *Statul în timpul și după Cantemir*, pp. 370-388 in Dogaru Mircea, Ciobanu Viorel, *Dimitrie Cantemir și conștiința unității românilor. Studii și articole dedicate Centenarului Marii Uniri*, Universul Academic Publishing House, Bucharest, 2018.
42. Tudosescu, Ion, *Acțiune umană și existență*. Fundația România de Mâine Publishing House, Bucharest, 2018.
43. Tudosescu, Ion, *Sistem social și acțiune umană. Expozeu de filosofie umană*, Fundația România de Mâine Publishing House, Bucharest, 2008.
44. Wright, Georg Henrick von, *Logica deontică și teoria generală a acțiunii* in *Norme, valori, acțiune. Analiza logică a discursului practic, cu aplicații în etică și în drept*, Text selection, translation and introductory study by Sorin Vieru, Dragan Stoianovici, Politica Publishing House, Bucharest, 1979.
45. Wright, Georg Henrick von, *Norm and action: A Logical Enquiry*, Routledge and Kegan Paul, London 1963.

PUBLIC INTEREST: CHALLENGES AND POSSIBILITIES IN IDENTIFYING THE CONTENT OF THIS NOTION[1]

LECTURER OANA ȘARAMET[2]

Abstract: *It is public administration that, through the exercise of its particular tasks, must respond to the needs of those communities in which it exercises competence. In any community, a multitude of general interests can be identified that would desirably be realized by the authorities and institutions of public administration. Unfortunately, most of the time, it is practically impossible to realize them all at the same time. The financial resources available to public administration are, as a rule, the main factor preventing the realization of all these legitimate public interests, even if they are identified in an objective way. As a result, it is necessary to prioritize certain interests, the realization of some becoming a priority over others. The public interest is a concept used in public administration for which it is difficult to construct a unanimously accepted definition and with much of the field appreciating that such a definition cannot be formulated. However, we believe that some defining elements of this legal concept can be identified, as well as some steps and principles that can be followed in public administration in order to identify the hierarchy of public interests that need to be satisfied in a community. As such, public administration will be forced to consider, and prioritize, those public interests that must be realized because they respond to the needs of the community, rather than to the interests of its governors. In our approach, we use a number of methods, including those that are comparative, grammatical, logical, systemic, and*

---

[1] This work was undertaken within the LOABUN Project: "Legality-opportunity, the ratio between them in the administrative act and the identification of risk factors in order to ensure good administration". This project won the 2018 competition "Grants for interdisciplinary teams" launched by the Transylvania University of Brasov.

[2] Oana Șaramet: Faculty of Law, Transylvania University of Brasov, Romania, oana.saramet@unitbv.ro.

teleological, as well as some that are less common in the field of law, such as empirical and experimental methods, to analyze the theoretical and practical aspects relevant to the topic.

Keywords: *public interest, legitimate interest, features, principles and steps in identifying the public interest.*

JEL Clasiffication: K10, K23

1. Introduction

Picture a fictional city. Its mayor issues an authorization to build a mall at its centre. At the moment that the construction of this mall is completed and put to use, due to the nature of its "geographical architecture", the construction and arrangement of the roads in the area and the circulation of means of transport, both public and private, will become "a mission impossible", especially when there is heavy traffic. Connecting between different neighborhoods, using any type of vehicle, will require a lot of patience and waste the time of any person who is in traffic because it is not possible to widen the road and a new one needs to be constructed. In this context, what public interest would a competent public administration authority identify in order to authorize such construction? Certainly, new jobs will emerge and investors and traders will come to the city, increasing revenues and local budgets, and the residents of the city or tourists will have a mall near them with all its amenities. But will the price paid by the vast majority of the city's inhabitants justify such construction? We can appreciate that, in this case, the public administration will correctly identify, without exceeding the limits of its discretionary power, the opportunity, if not the legality, of satisfying the public interest.

In an example from real life, an order by the Minister of Health[3] clarified that a child could benefit from special protection measures, including "special care and permanent supervision by another person" (in practical terms, one of the parents could act as a personal assistant of the child, therefore not depriving the family of an income if they gave up work to take care of their own child). This only applied to children between 0 and 7 suffering from type 1 diabetes, even though, according to the legal provisions in force at the time, childhood (the age of minority) was (and currently is) considered to cover the period between 0 and 18. At that time, it was more important for the Romanian state to reduce budgetary expenses, represented by the wages paid to parents who decided to stay at home to look after their children. It did not promote the best interests of the child.

However, in our opinion, the primary goal of public administration is to satisfy the public interest[4], thus ensuring good administration, and this includes "the proper functioning of the public administration as a system, with respect to clear, predictable rules, clearly known to those who carry out activities on behalf of the public administration, as well as by the citizens, and with the setting of public objectives that correspond to the

---

[3] This is about Order no. 725/12709/2002, as subsequently amended and supplemented, which was published in the Official Gazette, Part I, no. 781 on 28.10.2002. This order was issued by the Ministry of Health and Family and the National Authority for Child Protection and Adoption; it was repealed by Order no. 1306/1883/2015 for the approval of the biopsychosocial criteria for the classification of children with disabilities and the modalities of their application, published in the Official Gazette, Part I, no. 994 of 09.12.2016, after undergoing several changes. Following the proceedings at the National Council on Combating Discrimination, as well as those before the courts, these provisions have been modified without establishing a discriminatory regime. For more details, see: Ramona Lorena Paraschiv, *Copii cu diabet zaharat tip 1. Dreptul lor la sănătate, dreptul lor la viață: obligații pentru autorități*, article published at https://www.juridice.ro/458841/copii-cu-diabet-zaharat-tip-1-dreptul-lor-la-sanatate-dreptul-lor-la-viata-obligatii-pentru-autoritati.html, consulted on 1.10.2019 and Ramona Lorena Paraschiv, Oana Șaramet, *Theoretical and practical aspects regarding equality of rights and the right to health protection of children*, "Revista de Română de Drept European", Supplement to the International Conference Current Issues in the EU Political-Legal Space, third edition, October 27, 2016, pp. 205-212.

[4] Moreover, by art. 5 letter b) of the Administrative Code (this normative act was adopted by Emergency Ordinance no. 57/2019, published in the Official Gazette of Romania, Part I, no. 555 from 05.07.2019), the legislature appreciated that public administration refers to "the totality of activities carried out, under the regime of public power, of the organization and the execution of the law and the provision of public services, in order to satisfy the public interest".

wishes and needs of the latter”[5].

2. Aspects regarding the public interest. Identifying some defining elements and features of this concept

In accepting the constitutional norms of art. 21 and art. 52 of the Constitution of Romania, “the legitimate interest appears as a legal situation prior to subjective law, which prepares the terrain of subjective law, which is prefigured, appearing as a virtuality with a high degree of possibility, even certainty, being only a matter of time”[6].

The notion of the public interest designates the material and spiritual needs of a citizen in a single point[7]. Mircea Djuvara appreciates that not every interest generates a right, but rather only a moral, ideal interest, being the interest of social importance, which is useful to the community and of general interest[8]. The public interest, as well as other concepts such as public service, public order, and the public good, are concepts that depend on political purposes and whose meaning can change with changing political conceptions[9]. However, we do not consider that, in identifying the content of these concepts, it is just a matter of changing some political conceptions, but also of some moral, ethical, economic, and social transformations at the various levels of society, determining those at the political level[10].

The “dressing up in legal clothes”[11] of such concepts, by imposing a particular vision on them, is a desirable goal for any political force that

---

[5] Elisabeta Slabu, *Buna administrare în spațiul administrativ European*, summary of doctoral thesis accessible at: https://drept.unibuc.ro/dyn_doc/oferta-educationala/scoala-doctorala/rezumat-teza/rezumat2017SlabuElisabetaromana.pdf, consulted on 1.10.2019, p. 2.

[6] Antonie Iorgovan, *Tratat de drept administrativ*, vol. II, ed. All Beck, Bucharest, 2005, p. 562.

[7] Dana Apostol Tofan, *Drept administrativ*, vol. I, ed. C. H. Beck, Bucharest, 2014, p. 10.

[8] Mircea Djuvara, *Teoria generală a dreptului. Drept rațional. Izvoare și drept pozitiv*, Ed. All Beck, Bucharest, 1999, p. 128, *apud*. Mădălina Tomescu, *Interesul public*, ed. Pro Universitaria, Bucharest, 2014, p. 25.

[9] Antonie Iorgovan, *op. cit.*, p. 26.

[10] See in this regard Cătălin-Silviu Săraru, *Drept administrativ. Probleme fundamentale ale dreptului public*, C.H. Beck Publishing House, Bucharest, 2016, p. 28-31.

[11] Dana Apostol Tofan, *Drept administrativ*, vol. I, ed. C. H. Beck, Bucharest, 2018, p. 10.

enters government[12]. Even if the content of such a concept is supported by the majority who have brought the political force to power, it should not be assumed that this will not have an impact later on. This is why, based on the principle of transparent decision-making, any normative act that seeks to modify and/or supplement the content of such a concept should be the subject of public debate. Also, any attempt by local or national government to distort the content of such concepts by orienting them towards the satisfaction of private interests should be notified and even sanctioned by the political opposition and/or by an active civil society. Moreover, this doctrine notes that there must be no difference between the interests of the state (we could add to this the administrative-territorial unit) and the general interest, nor is language used that allows us to make such a distinction, meaning that a literal interpretation of the terms used must generate the same conclusion, namely, that the interest of the state (or even of the administrative-territorial unit) is closely identified with the public interest[13].

Those who govern thus exercise a true right of appreciation when deciding the content of such a concept by constructing a clear and precise definition, or by identifying its defining elements to guide those who apply the law. Moreover, doctrinal concepts such as those of public interest or the like, as mentioned above, are considered to fall into the category of indefinite legal concepts[14]. Such notions have "a broad and relatively determined meaning, the interpretation of which is left to the free choice of the ones called to apply the legal norm in which they are found"[15].

Indeed, as we have specified above, the legislature will, as a rule, be tempted to create a framework for identifying such a concept by specifying its essential aspects and identifiable parameters. In our opinion, this determines the concept to be either determinable or relatively determinate, but by no means indeterminate.

To consider it this way, in our opinion an indefinite concept[16] is

[12] See Dana Apostol Tofan, *Drept administrativ*, vol. I, *op. cit.*, 2018, p. 10.
[13] See in this regard Edwin Rekosh, *Who defines the public interest? Public Interest Law strategies in Central and Eastern Europe*, "PILI Papers", no. 1, July 2005, Columbia Law School, p. 10.
[14] Dana Apostol Tofan, *Drept administrativ*, vol. I *op. cit.*, 2018, p. 12.
[15] Ibid.
[16] Moreover, it should be noted in the doctrine that, starting from the fact that this concept of public interest is devoid of empirical substance, those who design and plan public policies, and how and when these policies are realized, have abandoned the public interest to the detriment of the public through the use of more "objective" criteria, such as cost-benefit and system analysis. Richard E. Klosterman, *A public interest criterion*, "Journal of the American Planning Association", July 1980, p. 323.

undesirable, because there would be the risk of not establishing the appropriate "coordinates" that those who apply the law can use to identify the general interest.

Moreover, the legislative body, through art. 2 paragraph (1), letter r) of Law no. 554/2004 with subsequent amendments and additions, identified elements of the rule of law that qualify the legitimate public interest[17]. These elements are: the order of law and constitutional democracy; the guarantee of rights, freedoms and fundamental duties of citizens; meeting community needs; and ensuring the competence of public authorities.

With regard to this definition, we consider that some clarification is required:

- The legal text speaks of legitimate public interest (in fact, when it referring to private interest, the ordinary legislature only targets legitimate interest), the options available to the ordinary legislature being determined, first of all, by the constitutional assembly who, both through the provisions of art. 21 and those of art. 52 of the constitution, considers only legitimate interests[18]. Why legitimate? Because "the fundamental law and the other laws do not defend and guarantee all interests, but only those which are based on law, custom, generally the sources of law"[19]. By recognizing the possibility of any person to address the institutions of justice in order to defend their legitimate interests, the constitutional provisions of art. 21 "did not put a condition of admissibility on the action in the court, but obligated justice to protect only legitimate interests"[20]. Taking this idea into account, we consider that the protection of legitimate interests should also be entrusted to the authorities and institutions of public administration who, within the limits of their competence, must identify public interests and pursue their protection at the level of the community in which their competence is exercised.

---

[17] Regarding administrative litigation having as its basis legitimate public interest see Cătălin-Silviu Săraru, *Contenciosul administrativ român*, C. H. Beck Publishing House, Bucharest, 2019, p. 199-203.

[18] From the point of view of legal significance, the notion of legitimate interest does not benefit from any detailed determination, because the practice of the courts is not a unitary one, and also because the optics of the doctrine are not a unitary one. See Ioan Muraru, Elena Simina Tănăsescu (coord.), *Constituția României. Comentariu pe articole*, ed. C. H. Beck, Bucharest, 2008, pp. 517-518; also Ana Rozalia Lazăr, *Reforma justiției și conteciosul administrativ,* "Curierul Judiciar" no. 5/2003, p. 10 et seq., *apud.* Ioan Muraru, Elena Simina Tănăsescu (coord.), *op. cit.*, p. 518.

[19] Ioan Muraru, Elena Simina Tănăsescu (coord.), *op. cit.*, p. 178.

[20] Ibid.

- By the provisions of art. 52 of the constitution, the constituent legislature has asserted one of the two guarantees enshrined in the fundamental laws of the country. This is the right to petition, i.e. the right of a person injured by a public authority, being nothing more than "the constitutional basis of the defense of citizens against the abuses of public authorities and, implicitly, of their responsibility for the damages caused to citizens"[21]. By exercising this right, citizens can defend themselves not only when their rights have been impinged upon through administrative acts by the authorities of public administration, but they can also defend their legitimate interests.

- Through these provisions, the constituent legislature has outlined the configuration of the legal framework necessary for the exercise of these fundamental rights. First of all, a citizen has the right seek redress of an injury not just in connection to a right, but also to a legitimate interest, which can be appreciated as a first step towards embracing the approach of European Union law, which "does not distinguish between legitimate interest and, rightly, the existence of a direct connection between the individual and the act that damages them is sufficient to be notified"[22].

- What is this legitimate interest? In this legal doctrine, in order for an interest to be considered we must ask:

➢ Whether it is necessary or not to contravene the legal order in force[23];

➢ so as to find its source and to be protected by a legal norm[24].

- We also appreciate[25] that the constituent legislature wanted, through the constitutional revision of 2003, to offer the individual a wider sphere of situations in which a person can engage in administrative litigation and for this reason, considering not only the violation of subjective rights, but also of legitimate interests. The acceptance that any

---

[21] Antonie Iorgovan, *Tratat de drept administrativ*, vol. I, Ed. All Beck, Bucharest, 2005, p. 66.

[22] Ioan Muraru, Elena Simina Tănăsescu (coord.), *op. cit.*, p. 518.

[23] See in this regard Tudor Drăganu, *Liberul acces la justiţie*, Ed. Lumina Lex, Bucharest, 2003, p. 86, *apud.* Rodica Narcisa Petrescu, *Drept administrativ*, Ed. Hamangiu, Bucharest, 2009, p. 438. For criticism of these claims see Dacian Cosmin Dragoş, *Implicaţiile revizuirii Constituţiei asupra contenciosului administrativ: discuţii privind semnificaţia sintagmei "interes legitim"*, "Revista Transilvană de Ştiinţe Administrative", 2 (11), 2004, p. 17 et seq.

[24] See in this regard Tudor Drăganu, *op. cit*, 2003, p. 86. Antonie Iorgovan, *Tratat de drept administrativ*, vol. I, Ed. All Beck, Bucharest, 2002, p. 509. For criticism of these claims see Dacian Cosmin Dragoş, *op. cit.*, 2004, p. 17 et seq.

[25] See in this regard Dacian Cosmin Dragoş, *op. cit.*, 2004, p. 34.

legitimate interest has the "quality of not being against the law, of not protecting an illegal or immoral situation"[26] was also considered.

- Although, in this context, we focus on the public interest and on issues related to it, we cannot ignore that the legislature does not expressly distinguish between public and private interest, rather referring only to legitimate interest. This constitutional approach causes us to find that any provision in our legislation, including in the area of administrative law, only concerns legitimate interests, no matter whether public or private: legitimacy is a trait specific to both forms of interest[27].

- Romania's ordinary legislature also defined legitimate private interest through art. 2 paragraph (1) letter p) of Law no. 554/2004, with subsequent modifications and additions, considering the achievement of a future and predictable subjective right.

- The legal consecration of the possibility of an injured person to defend a legitimate public interest makes possible, implicitly, the legal recognition of an objective litigation, while the defense of a legitimate private interest implies a subjective litigation[28].

- In French administrative law, which inspired the Romanian legislature, administrative litigation focuses primarily on two types of litigation: an appeal against an entity acting in excess of its power and a litigant having full jurisdiction[29]. An appeal on an excess of power has an objective character, with the judge verifying the objective legality of the act[30]. The judge will annul the act if he finds it to be illegal in order to restore objective legality, and not to repair the damage caused to the applicant, while the public administration, issuing the act, will defend such an administrative act[31].

In contrast, a litigant having full jurisdiction allows the judge to verify, in substance, the subjective legality of the administrative act[32]. If

---

[26] Ibid.

[27] French jurisprudence reached the conclusion that "the interests likely to be invoked by the judicial appeal may be: purely moral—aimed at obtaining only moral satisfactions by annulling the administrative act; personal or individual; collective—targeting the common interest sustained by several natural persons organized or not in a legal form of association, such as an association, a foundation or a union and which is not confused with the public interest for the protection of which public authorities or institutions can act". See in this regard Dacian Cosmin Dragoș, *op. cit.*, 2004, p. 19.

[28] Dana Apostol Tofan, *Drept administrativ*, vol. I, *op. cit.*, 2018, p. 164.

[29] Dacian Cosmin Dragoș, *op. cit.*, 2004, p. 18.

[30] *Idem*, pp. 18-19.

[31] See Dacian Cosmin Dragoș, *op. cit.*, 2004, p. 18

[32] *Idem*, p. 19.

its illegality is found, the court will annul, replace, or modify the act, and also establish pecuniary sanctions for the repair of any damage if necessary[33].

Therefore, through an appeal on an excess power, the court intervenes to cancel an administrative act issued or adopted by a public administration in excess of its power, exercising its right of discretionary assessment. In the case of this form of appeal, the existence of the interest on which to take legal action (of procedural interest) and the objective legality of the administrative act must be proved. In a case on full jurisdiction, the plaintiff wishes to defend a subjective right against injury. The existence of such injury will have to be proved and so, implicitly, will the procedural interest.

In the provisions of art. 52 of the constitution, as well as those of Law no. 554/2004 with subsequent amendments and additions, it can be observed that the legislature did not make such a distinction because, following an action in an administrative dispute pursued by an injured person either in defence of a right or a legitimate interest, by a public authority through an administrative act or an act under its purview, this person is entitled not only to request and obtain recognition of the right or legitimate interest claimed, through the cancellation of the act, but also to repair any damage. Therefore, a case with full jurisdiction is established when it is based on a subjective right, as well as when it is based on a legitimate interest.

- From the aforementioned, it appears that a legitimate interest as the subject of a legal action should not be confused with the interest of acting in court, the latter having to be proved when the action aims to protect a subjective right.

- Starting from such aspects of jurisprudence, the doctrine also identifies certain features that must be present in order to confer the quality of legal action[34]. Such features have also been identified by another author who offers a definition of the notion of legitimate interest. He specifies that it is a personal interest, direct and current, in accordance with the general interest and the rules of social coexistence, but without yet having legal protection in the sense of the fullness of a right recognized by law[35]. Regarding the proposed definition, we consider it appropriate to offer some clarification. In the way the definition is formulated, it seems obvious to us that it is, in fact, a more appropriate definition of a legitimate private

---

[33] *Idem*, p. 18.

[34] *Idem*, pp. 19-20.

[35] Ana Rozalia Lazăr, *Legalitatea actului administrativ. Drept românesc şi comparat*, ed. All Beck, Bucharest, 2004, p. 46.

interest, because the public interest should be identified with the general interest, and therefore does not have to agree with itself. In our opinion, the relevant features in this could be as follows[36]:

- the interest must be real or, at least partially real—as it is when a person wrongly considers that an administrative act is unfavorable to him/her, such as when an act concerns several categories of persons, but a claim is made by only one person;
- the interest must be personal to the person invoking it, whether in terms of private or public interest;
- the interest must be relevant and the relevance is indicated by the link between the interest invoked and the administrative act challenged;
- the interest must directly concern the administrative act in question;
- and, of course, the interest must be certain.

Alongside legal will, interest is the essence of law[37]. Therefore, interest, and we may only consider legitimate interest, is a legal situation prior to subjective law, prefiguring a subjective right, and preceding and preparing for the appearance of this right.

As such, when we analyze an interest we must not use a one-dimensional approach[38]. We should keep in mind that "a moral interest, an ideal, of social importance, useful to the community, that is, the general interest is one that generates the right"[39], as mentioned previously. But not all interests generate law and there may be interests that do not determine the appearance of law, rules, legal norms or even rights[40]. It is also necessary to identify them in order to protect those legitimate interests—public and private—that we wish to achieve by applying the created law.

3. Possible steps for identifying the public interest

Legitimate public interest arouses wide discussion regarding its content. In terms of identifying the existence of such interests and qualifying more or less appropriate situations as being of public interest, it is obvious

---

[36] See Dacian Cosmin Dragoş, *op. cit.*, 2004, pp. 19-20.

[37] Nicolae Popa (coord.), *Teoria generală a dreptului. Caiet de seminar*, ed. C. H. Beck, Bucharest, 2014, p. 39.

[38] We could also talk about a third dimension in talking about a person's interest in taking legal action to defend your rights and/or legitimate interests.

[39] Mircea Djuvara, *op. cit.*, p. 128, *apud.* Mădălina Tomescu, *op. cit*, p. 25.

[40] Mircea Djuvara, *Precizări de filozofie juridică* in *Eseuri de filosofia dreptului*, ed. Trei, Bucharest, 1997, p. 23, *apud.* Mădălina Tomescu, *op. cit*, p. 26.

that this is "a fundamental concept for a government based on representative democracy and for good public administration"[41].

However, as we can see even from the definition of legitimate public interest given by the ordinary legislature, and which governors and other exponents of public administration frequently use in justifying their actions, the public interest is one of the most difficult concepts to define and perhaps one of the least understood[42]. This is why, in the concrete identification of practical situations that can be appreciated as being of public interest[43], difficulties, divergences, and different interpretations appear; however, these should not exceed the limits of reasonable assessment by the public administration[44].

As we have already mentioned, in order to identify this concept, with a fairly broad meaning and not restricting it to overly-precise limitations, it is appropriate to consider a structured procedure of several stages[45]. These steps would be:

- first, the relevant population should be identified, that is, the population whose interests need to be taken into account when making a

---

[41] Chris Wheeler, *The public interest. We know it's important, but do we know what it means*, "AIAL Forum" No. 48, 2006, p. 12.

[42] Ibid.

[43] An example of a case in which the court held that it was not a matter of prejudice to a legitimate interest, including a procedural interest in bringing proceedings, is as follows. By a decision of a county council, the election of its two vice-presidents was ascertained, and, according to the minutes, on that occasion it was stated that each political "arc" was requested to make two proposals. The representative of the applicant political group stated at that time that he had no proposal and subsequently voted to suspend the nominations. In fact, there were only two proposals and both were adopted so that there was no proposed person who was not chosen. Therefore, no matter whether the vote was to be held or not, they could only elect vice-presidents from among those who had applied. Consequently, the court considered that the applicant political party did not justify any interest in bringing the action because its admission would be of no practical use to it. If the vote were to resume, it could only concern the two nominations proposed because no illegality had been indicated prior to the time when the councilors voted on the candidacy (Pitesti Court of Appeal, commercial and administrative and fiscal litigation section, decision no. 2065/R-C of June 27, 2005, in *Curtea de Apel Piteşti, Buletinul jurisprudenţei*, 2005, ed. C. H. Beck, Bucharest, 2005, pp. 202-203, *apud.* Gabriela Bogasiu, *Legea contenciosului administrativ. Comentată şi adnotată*, ed. Universul Juridic, Bucharest, 2015, pp. 40-41).

[44] See Right to Life Association (NSW) Inc. v Secretary, Department of Human Services and Health (1995) 128 ALR 238 per Lockhart J, *apud.* Chris Wheeler, *op. cit.*, 2006, p. 15.

[45] See in this regard Chris Wheeler, *op. cit.*, 2006, p. 18.

decision;

- second, one should seek to identify the public interests that could be impacted by the question or decision;

- and third, each public interest identified, including through the balancing of public interests that might be in competition or even conflict, should be analyzed and weighed up, metaphorically speaking, with others.

Regarding the above mentioned steps, and to allow the identification of an interest as a public one, some clarification is required[46].

In other words, first of all, identifying the public interest should start from the needs of the respective community—needs that should also find a legal solution in relation to the legal acts of the public administration. The central point in identifying these public interests should by no means be the mere will of governors or administrative authorities.

Although it may apparently be easy to identify the population whose interests need to be taken into account, first deciding on them and then acting to protect them, the process can often prove to be both difficult and delicate in reality.

Any public administration will have to discover such issues by communicating with members of the relevant community. They can aim to discover any notable issue of public interest, including public interests that are desired to be realized or have already been realized by members of a community, through petitions and audiences, for example, or, conversely, by identifying them through political representatives such as local councilors or even civil servants, especially if the activities they carry out involve direct contact with community members. It is important, though, not just to identify public interests that need to be met, but those that fall within the competence of the public administration. Any public administration needs to be attentive to the needs of the community, engaging with those public interests that it wants to see fulfilled.

Once the various community and public interest components are identified, the public administration, especially that part that is responsible for the decision-making process, will have to identify those public interests that can be achieved given its legal competence and also that match the goals it has set, including those proposed under any recognizable discretionary power. Especially in the case of large communities, situations may arise where people may wish to satisfy a public interest, but the public administration cannot fulfill it due to a lack of financial and/or human resources, deficient infrastructure, or because it does not meet/correspond to policy objectives.

---

[46] *Idem*, p.18 et seq.

In identifying the objectives to be achieved because they are of public interest, a consistent role must be played not so much by public officials, i.e. those who hold an eligible or appointed function, but by civil servants. Indeed, at first glance, identifying public interests to be attained seems easy, because they can be identified through political platforms and proposals of candidates for public office during campaigns. These are certainly primary sources for discovering such public interests; but a civil servant will have to "certify", using his specified capacities, their legitimacy by referring to the relevant primary legislation. If there is no specific regulation, or it is stated only at the level of principle, then this must be done by reference to secondary legislation or even to those rules established at the level of the relevant public authority or institution. Nor can legislative provisions regarding the procedural steps to satisfy such general interests be ignored. This does not mean that a complex procedure will ensure the achievement of the proposed objectives; however, it will help prioritize them. Until a complex procedure is undertaken in order to reach a public interest objective, others requiring simplified procedures can be implemented.

In the objective identification of these public interests, and even in their ordering, it is necessary to take into account the relevant plans and policies identified at the level of a public authority or institution, or by any public authority hierarchically superior to or under its authority as the case may be. However, as long as such public interests are identified and prioritized in an objective way, in compliance with all relevant legal aspects, their existence and/or their realization should not be affected by the changing political hue of those elected or appointed. Their right of appreciation must be "coordinated" by the aspects of legality, objectivity and impartiality in the consideration of an interest as being legitimately public, not by their political or private wishes.

On the other hand, most of the time it is possible to identify several public interests that could desirably be satisfied, but the public administration will, as a rule, be unable to fulfill them all at once. Thus, it will be necessary to prioritize them and the doctrine even specifies the possibility of selecting between identified public interests and those to be realized on the basis of a compromise[47] to which the public administration and those administered by it must come. Moreover, in this case we find the statement that "sometimes it is more appropriate to choose the least bad option—the decision that produces the least evil, than the one that produces the greatest good"[48]. In ranking these competing public interests, a number

[47] See in this regard Chris Wheeler, *op. cit.*, 2006, p. 21.
[48] Ibid.

of criteria should be considered, such as: the legal framework available for the procedural steps needed to satisfy a legitimate or other public interest; the financial and human resources available to the administration in order to achieve them, or to which it can appeal by the conclusion of public contracts; the rights and/or legitimate private interests affected; and the number of people affected when a public interest can no longer be realized. We also appreciate, however, that the way in which a community is affected[49] by the definitive or temporary realization of an interest is the most important factor that a decision-making administration must take into consideration.

Extrapolating doctrinal support, we can appreciate that the public administration displays virtue if its actions are in accordance with the public interest, that is, its actions lead to the realization of such an interest, and not to the violation of the peace and good order of society. This is in the context of a framework that makes it possible for individuals to successfully pursue their own interests[50]. Thus, even the virtuous individual will be able to act in a virtuous way in order to achieve his own goals and, in doing so, he will contribute, in different ways, to the realization of the public interest by the public administration[51]. Moreover, the public interest does not provide instructions on how to live and to act, but rather it offers a space in which to act[52].

4. Principles to guide the process of identifying the public interest

In order to identify the public interest, several "governing" principles have been proposed[53]. We think these principles should guide this process:

- The principle of participation. It is essential to democracy that people are allowed to participate in public debates and to make the public

---

[49] Ibid.

[50] See Stuart D. Warner, *David Hume on the public interest*, "Reason Papers. A Journal of Interdisciplinary Normative Studies": Essays to Commemorate the 250th Anniversary of the Completion of David Hume's A treatise of Human Nature, no. 15, Summer 1990, p. 89.

[51] Ibid.

[52] Ibid.

[53] Jean-François Méthot, *How to define public interest?*, lecture held at EPAC Round-Table, Saint Paul University, 29 January 2003, Ottawa, Canada, pp. 2-4, https://ustpaul.ca/upload-files/EthicsCenter/activities-How_to_Define_Public_Interest.pdf, consulted on 10.10.2019.

interests that they wish to be realized known, because "they are the ones who ensure the foundation of political power and legitimize the distinction between the governors and the governed"[54].

- The principle of charity (goodwill, good faith), according to which whenever we give an interpretation to a statement, if a decision generates an obvious state of contradiction or confusion then it is necessary to identify another reasonable interpretation. To justify why, as a result of prioritizing public interests, some are realized sooner than others, it is necessary for the administration to find the most appropriate way to justify a decision. The resources that will be used to achieve some of these interests are to the detriment of others and people may not consider them a priority.

- The principle of subsidiarity, according to which decisions on the appropriate identification of public interests and their prioritization must be taken into account so as to best correspond to the needs of the communities involved.

- The principle of autonomy, according to which, while respecting the fundamental values of the state, as well as the fundamental laws of the state, by identifying public interests that are to be realized, the governors do not have to impose other values on the community.

- The principle of transparency. This is a fundamental principle in any democracy, according to which the administration must be transparent not only as regards the public interests to be realized, but also as regards the entire decision-making process used to identify these public interests.

5. Conclusions

The public interest, and similar concepts such as "the general welfare" and "the common good", have played an important role in the works of many authors ranging from Plato and Aristotle to Locke, Rousseau and Marx. This term appears, with regularity, in legislative debates and in legal regulations, and has gained a particular contemporary relevance, especially in terms of the public interests of consumers and those in the field of environmental protection, but also through the political actions of different groups in society[55].

"The public interest is somewhere between the political and the social because the state, as the main political organization of the society, aims to promote and guarantee the general interests of the society from which they were born, to be achieved through multiple internal and external

[54] *Idem*, p. 3.
[55] Richard E. Klosterman, *op. cit.*, p. 323.

functions of the state"[56]. Any administrative act must be issued by the public administration in the public interest or, in other words, the lawful cause of any administrative act is represented by the satisfaction of a public interest[57]. Therefore, when the public administration is given the freedom to act, this is not recognized as being absolute in the sense that it is allowed to act exclusively as it decides, but to best serve the public interest[58]. This is why we should be most concerned about who is involved in defining the public interest and by what means; not just about finding out what the public interest is[59].

Synthesizing the above, we appreciate that, in identifying an interest to be satisfied by the public administration, it is necessary for the legislature to consider legitimate interests only, be they public or private. This refers to any interest that does not contravene the law and which protects a legal or moral situation. Implicitly, this also refers to the authority of the public administration or a public institution that organizes the execution of the law, but also the concrete execution of the law and it will have to take into account only this interest. Then, in order for an interest to be regarded as a public, it is necessary to identify its features, namely: that it is real or, at least partially real; that it is personally relevant to the person invoking it; that it is directly affected by the administrative act under appeal; and that it is clear and certain.

We consider that identifying an interest as a legitimate public interest is a process that should go through the following steps: identifying the relevant population, being the population whose interests should be taken into account in making the decision; identifying public interests that might be of concern in such a decision; and analyzing and balancing competing or conflicting public interests in order to prioritize them. If we are dealing with competing public interests, a number of criteria should be considered, such as: the legal framework available to take the procedural steps to satisfy a legitimate public interest; the financial and human resources available to the administration in order to achieve it or to which it can appeal; the rights and/or legitimate private interests affected; and the number of people who would be affected if that public interest were no longer realized.

---

[56] Mădălina Tomescu, *op. cit.,* p. 30-31.
[57] Ovidiu Podaru, *Drept administrativ. Practică judiciară comentată. Vol. I. Actul administrativ (II). Un secol de jurisprudență (1909-2009)*, Ed. Hamagiu, Bucharest, 2010, p. 269.
[58] See Ovidiu Podaru, *op. cit.*, p. 269.
[59] Edwin Rekosh, *op. cit.*, p. 11.

Bibliography

1. Ana Rozalia Lazăr, *Legalitatea actului administrativ. Drept românesc şi comparat*, ed. All Beck, Bucharest, 2004.
2. Ana Rozalia Lazăr, *Reforma justiţiei şi conteciosul administrativ*, "Curierul Judiciar" no. 5/2003.
3. Antonie Iorgovan, *Tratat de drept administrativ*, vol. I and II, ed. All Beck, Bucharest, 2005.
4. Cătălin-Silviu Săraru, *Contenciosul administrativ român*, C. H. Beck Publishing House, Bucharest, 2019.
5. Cătălin-Silviu Săraru, *Drept administrativ. Probleme fundamentale ale dreptului public*, C. H. Beck Publishing House, Bucharest, 2016.
6. Chris Wheeler, *The public interest. We know it's important, but do we know what it means*, "AIAL Forum" No. 48, 2006.
7. Dacian Cosmin Dragoş, *Implicaţiile revizuirii Constituţiei asupra contenciosului administrativ: discuţii privind semnificaţia sintagmei "interes legitim*", "Revista Transilvană de Ştiinţe Administrative", 2 (11), 2004.
8. Dana Apostol Tofan, *Drept administrativ*, vol. I, ed. C. H. Beck, Bucharest, 2018.
9. Edwin Rekosh, *Who defines the public interest? Public Interest Law strategies in Central and Eastern Europe*, "PILI Papers", no. 1, July 2005, Columbia Law School.
10. Gabriela Bogasiu, *Legea contenciosului administrativ. Comentată şi adnotată*, ed. Universul Juridic, Bucharest, 2015.
11. Ioan Muraru, Elena Simina Tănăsescu (coord.), *Constituţia României. Comentariu pe articole*, ed. C. H. Beck, Bucharest, 2008.
12. Jean-François Méthot, *How to define public interest?*, lecture held at EPAC Round-Table, Saint Paul University, 29 January 2003, Ottawa, Canada, https://ustpaul.ca/upload-files/EthicsCenter/activities-How _to_Define_ Public_Interest.pdf, consulted on 10.10.2019.
13. Mădălina Tomescu, *Interesul public*, ed. Pro Universitaria, Bucharest, 2014.
14. Mircea Djuvara, *Precizări de filozofie juridică în Eseuri de filosofia dreptului*, ed. Trei, Bucharest, 1997.
15. Mircea Djuvara, *Teoria generală a dreptului. Drept raţional. Izvoare şi drept pozitiv*, Ed. All Beck, Bucharest, 1999.
16. Nicolae Popa (coord.), *Teoria generală a dreptului. Caiet de seminar*, ed. C. H. Beck, Bucharest, 2014.
17. Ovidiu Podaru, *Drept administrativ. Practică judiciară comentată. Vol. I. Actul administrativ (II). Un secol de jurisprudenţă (1909-*

2009), Ed. Hamagiu, Bucharest, 2010.
18. Ramona Lorena Paraschiv, Oana Șaramet, *Theoretical and practical aspects regarding equality of rights and the right to health protection of children*, "Revista de Română de Drept European", Supplement to the International Conference Current Issues in the EU Political-Legal Space, third edition, October 27, 2016, pp. 205-212.
19. Richard E. Klosterman, *A public interest criterion*, "Journal of the American Planning Association", July 1980.
20. Rodica Narcisa Petrescu, *Drept administrativ*, Ed. Hamangiu, Bucharest, 2009.
21. Stuart D. Warner, *David Hume on the public interest*, "Reason Papers. A Journal of Interdisciplinary Normative Studies": Essays to Commemorate the 250th Anniversary of the Completion of David Hume's A treatise of Human Nature, no. 15, Summer 1990.
22. Tudor Drăganu, *Liberul acces la justiție*, Ed. Lumina Lex, Bucharest, 2003.

Part II.

Administrative Codification in Comparative Law

DECONCENTRATED PUBLIC SERVICES ACCORDING TO THE ADMINISTRATIVE CODE

PROFESSOR VERGINIA VEDINAȘ[1]
PHD. IOAN LAURENȚIU VEDINAȘ[2]

Abstract: *This study analyzes, on the one hand, how the Administrative Code regulates the decentralized public services of ministries and other authorities of the specialized central administration and, on the other hand, the changes made in this regulation in relation to Law no. 340/2004, as repealed in this normative act. We ascertain that there is now a more complete and systematic regulation of this category of public institutions, regulated at the constitutional level through art. 123 paragraph (1), which qualifies the prefect as head of these services. Indirectly, they are also targeted by art. 120 paragraph (1), which places among the constitutional principles of organization and functioning of the local public administration the principle of deconcentrating public services. Analysis is made regarding the heads of decentralized public services, for whom the Administrative Code regulates by statute, both public servants in management positions and employees under individual employment contracts and management contracts.*

Keywords: *decentralized public services, prefect, decentralization, public administration, administrative law.*

JEL Classification: *K23*

[1] Verginia Vedinaș, Faculty of Law, University of Bucharest, Romania, prof.verginia.vedinas@gmail.com.

[2] Ioan Laurențiu Vedinaș, dodo_emre9@yahoo.com

1. Constitutional regulation of the deconcentration of public services and of decentralized public services[3]

The Romanian Constitution, as revised and republished, contains two categories of provision that have applicability in the issue analyzed here. These are, firstly, provisions regarding the principles according to which local public administration is organized and functions, including the deconcentration of public services. The applicability of the constitutional norm regarding this principle is highlighted by the fact that the decentralized public services of ministries and other specialized bodies of the central administration represent subjects of public law through which this principle of deconcentration is realized.

The second is represented by art. 123 paragraph (1), which deals with the chief prefect of the decentralized public services of ministries and other specialized bodies of the central administration.

Deconcentration, as a principle of local public administration, is currently defined by the Administrative Code[4] in art. 5, which contains general definitions applicable to public administration. Among them, u) stipulates that deconcentration represents the "distribution of administrative and financial attributions from the level of the central public administration by the ministries and other specialized bodies of the central public administration to the specialized structures of the administration in territorial-administrative units".

The paradox of the Administrative Code is that, although deconcentration is placed among the "general definitions applicable to public administration", and, especially, despite the constitution stating in art. 120 paragraph (1) that it is the first principle of organization and functioning of the local public administration, it is no longer found among the principles provided by art. 75 of the Administrative Code as being "specific to local public administration".

We note that this text includes the principles of: decentralization; local autonomy; the consultation of citizens and solving problems of local interest; the eligibility of public administration authorities; and cooperation, responsibility, and the principle of budget constraint.

---

[3] On the deconcentration of public services see Verginia Vedinaș, *Tratat teoretic și practic de drept administrativ*, vol. I, Universul Juridic Publishing House, Bucharest, 2018, p. 302-304; Cătălin-Silviu Săraru, *Drept administrativ. Probleme fundamentale ale dreptului public*, C. H. Beck Publishing House, Bucharest, 2016, p. 663, 664.

[4] See Government Emergency Ordinance no. 57/2019 regarding the Administrative Code, published in the Official Gazette, Part I no. 555 of July 5, 2019, as amended.

We note also that, in the sphere of the principles enshrined in the Administrative Code, on the one hand, the principle of deconcentrating public services is lacking, and on the other, three other principles have been added, which the previous Law no. 215/2001 did not foresee in terms of the principles of cooperation, responsibility and budgetary constraint.

We conclude that the lack of decentralization of public services, in terms of the principles that govern local public administration, is a real deficiency that needs to be eliminated in the future. Its source lies in the conception that gives priority to decentralization, which desires to increase the prerogatives of autonomous local authorities to consolidate true "local democracies". However, this principle should not be absolute, but correlated with other principles that govern the organization of the administration as a whole.

In this context, we specify that, according to art. 10, a general principle applicable to public administration is the principle of satisfying the public interest, which means, on the one hand, the satisfaction of the public interest before that of the individual or group, and, on the other hand, the priority of national public interest over local public interest.

2. Deconcentrated public services according to the Administrative Code

Provisions regarding this matter can be found in Part IV of the Administrative Code entitled "the prefect, the prefect's institution and decentralized public services". This substantially took over the content of Law no. 340/2004, of the same title, but, at the same time, also provides a regulatory supplement in Title II devoted to this matter.

Deconcentrated public services can be set up by ministries, but also by the other specialized bodies of the central public administration, including various agencies, offices, inspectorates, authorities, and guards. For example, the National Authority for Consumer Protection (ANPC) has decentralized services in each county and in the municipality of Bucharest, according to its law of organization and functioning, which are termed regional commissariats for consumer protection, as well as the National Centre for Testing and Product Expertise (LAREX).

From the point of view of the name of these decentralized public services, we encounter the same terminological diversity, similar to those by which the authorities establishing them are invoked. In some cases, both the authority of the specialized central administration and its decentralized service are covered by the same name (for example: The National Authority for Tax Administration (ANAF) has decentralized services bearing this name, supplemented by specifying the region in which they are constituted, or, in the case of Bucharest, the relevant sector).

After 1990, in some areas decentralized public services were set up by region, seeing several counties being covered by such services. Even the authorities already mentioned, the ANAF and ANPC, have regional structures as part of their composition. I have never been in favour of this solution, as I consider it to have introduced a "backdoor" to an administrative-territorial unit, i.e. the region, which the Romanian Constitution does not provide. Moreover, the constitution of these regional structures also had a profoundly illegitimate motivation—the aim was to consolidate the individuality of certain regions or "lands" on the basis of ethnic criteria. We refer here, in particular, to those occupied by the Hungarian ethnicity and evoked by terms such as "Ţinutul Secuiesc (Szeklerland)" or "Har-Cov", the abbreviation of the two counties that constitute "the region" (Harghita and Covasna).

Equally, it should be taken into account that, according to art. 123 paragraph (2) of the constitution, the prefect conducts decentralized public services from territorial administrative units. The notion of territorial administrative units must be related to those provided in art. 3 paragraph (3) of the constitution, according to which "the territory is organized, in the administrative aspect, in communes, cities and counties. According to the law, some cities are declared municipalities". We find in the constitutional text that the "region" is, in fact, not recognized as an administrative-territorial unit at the constitutional level. This presents a problem: if such regional decentralized public services are constituted, how will their prefectures be managed? Furthermore, which prefect will lead such a service? What happens and what are the prefect's colleagues doing?

As we have already mentioned, decentralized services are regulated under Title II in Part IV of the Administrative Code.

The functions of deconcentrated public services fall into three categories relating to the control, inspection and monitoring in a ministry's field of activity or of the specialized body of the central public administration in which it operates.

Reports of subordination and management of the decentralized public services show the peculiarity exercised by two categories of legal subject. First, that exercised by the relevant ministries and other competent specialized bodies of the central public administration, whose management, which we can qualify vertically, is materialized in:

a) establishing the organizational chart, the number of positions, and the management functions of the decentralized public services in their purview;

b) issuing orders and instructions that are mandatory for subordinated public services.

The second legal subject for which the constitution recognizes leadership prerogatives, and which we can describe as being horizontal, is the prefect. Article 279 paragraph (3) of the Administrative Code stipulates that "the prefect conducts and coordinates the activity of decentralized public services at county level, in order to ensure the implementation of measures in the government program and in situations involving the emergency intervention of state bodies in the territory".

We can see, from the interpretation of these provisions, that there are two types of leadership activity that the prefect performs: the one in ordinary, normal situations, which seeks the translation into practice of the government program and the one in special situations, which imposes intervention by state bodies.

In carrying out this double mission, the prefect fulfills the powers that art. 254 of the Administrative Code gives in order to fulfill the constitutional role of leading decentralized public services[5].

The Administrative Code establishes, by art. 279 paragraph (4), the principle of collaboration between the prefect, on the one hand, and the ministries and other organs of the central specialized administration, on the other, in leading public services decentralized from administrative-territorial units.

We specify that the text stipulates the obligation of the two categories of public authority, the prefect and bodies of the central

---

[5] Art. 254 of the Administrative Code has the following content: "*Attributions in the exercise of the constitutional role of leading decentralized public services. In exercising the attributions provided for in art. 252 para. (1) letter b), the prefect: a) verifies, under the conditions of art. 259, the way in which decentralized public services of ministries and other central public administration bodies fulfill their monitoring and control tasks in the field in which they operate; b) approves the budgets and financial statements regarding the budgetary execution of the decentralized public services of ministries and of other central public administration bodies subordinated to the Government and sends them to the head of the institution hierarchically superior to the decentralized public service. The opinions are consultative in nature; c) may propose to the minister or, respectively, to the head of a public administration body, under which these public services carry out the disciplinary investigation of the deconcentrated public service leader, if he considers that he has committed, in connection with the performance of his duties, a fact that constitutes a disciplinary offense or, as the case may be, it may refer directly to the competent discipline committee; d) may appoint by order a representative of the prefect's institution in the competition commission for the position of manager of a public service decentralized from the county*".

specialized administration, to collaborate in order to exercise legal prerogatives regarding the management of decentralized public services.

We appreciate that this gives rise to rights and correlative obligations to inform each other and to maintain a permanent connection in order to carry out both their own management duties and those that involve both subjects. In fact, in our opinion, this collaboration must be a permanent aspect of the relationship.

The code not only establishes the principle of collaboration, but also ways for this collaboration to materialize, such as mandatory communication between prefects, ministries and other specialized bodies of the central administration, of the normative acts they have issued in areas that fall within the scope of activity of decentralized public services, for which the law does not provide through publication in the Official Gazette.

We interpret that these must be different administrative acts emanating from the specialized central administration to the orders and instructions that are compulsorily published in the Official Gazette, according to Law no. 24/2000 regarding the norms of legislative technique, but also the provisions of art. 57 paragraph (3) of the Administrative Code, according to which "The administrative acts of normative character, not classified, according to the law, issued by ministers, are published in the Official Gazette of Romania, part I".

It follows, from the corroboration of the two categories of provisions, that the normative acts of ministries and other specialized bodies of the central public administration are classified and submitted to the prefect.

A regulation that we are convinced will bring about many problems in practice concerns the status of the leaders of decentralized public services. From an analysis of art. 280 of the Administrative Code[6], it is clear that these may be: a public civil servant; contract staff with an

---

[6] Art. 280 has the following content: "*Appointment and dismissal of the heads of decentralized public services. (1) The manager of the decentralized public service holding a public management position shall be appointed and released from office by order of the relevant minister or the head of the specialized body of the competent central public administration. The order shall be communicated to the prefect of the county in which the decentralized public service is organized or has the headquarters or prefect of the Bucharest municipality, as the case may be, within 10 days from their intervention. (2) The manager of the decentralized public service that has the status of employee with an individual employment contract or the quality of an employee with a management contract concluded under the conditions of the law fulfills his powers under the conditions stipulated in the concluded contract. (3) The manager of the decentralized public service has the capacity of an authorizing credit officer*".

individual employment contract (employees); and contract staff with a management contract.

We are concerned about the reasons for such diversity, which causes us to ask under what criteria will some of these leaders have one status while others will have another? Who decides this and, in particular, what will happen in practice?

It is known that the heads of decentralized services have always been in the political spotlight, as it is the politicians who enjoy the freedom to decide who runs these services and act accordingly. In this respect, Government Emergency Ordinance no. 37/2009[7] addressed some measures to improve public administration and excluded management officials from heading up decentralized public services[8]. This was declared unconstitutional by the Constitutional Court, but, unfortunately, there were many negative effects when it was in force and, especially, when it was not.

We find that the same thing happens in decentralized services at the county level, where the presidents of the county councils undergo all kinds of procedures in order to be able to place in the leadership of these services those they prefer and removing those who already occupy these positions.

Therefore, we consider that the solution in relation to the Administrative Code regarding the status of the heads of these services, instead of diminishing the phenomenon, will aggravate it.

3. Conclusions

We have aimed to make a brief presentation of the regulation of decentralized public services under the Administrative Code. These services have a special significance in the life of the country and of local authorities, because, as the prefect is the representative of the government in a territory and the correspondent of the prime minister in a county, so are the decentralized public services and the representatives of ministries and other authorities of the central specialized administration, and their leaders correspond to ministers at county level. Therefore, good regulation of these services and their managers influences the quality of their activity. We hope that, regarding the heads of these services, their legal status will be clarified by the law in line with the Administrative Code.

---

[7] Published in the Official Gazette no. 264 / April 22, 2009, rejected by Law no. 41/2010, published in the Official Gazette no. 170/16 March 2010.

[8] For a critical analysis of this ordinance, see Verginia Vedinas, *Mutații aduse în statutul funcționarilor publici prin O.U.G. nr. 37/2009,* in volume *Liber amicorum Nicolae Popa,* Hamangiu Publishing House, Bucharest, 2009, pp. 249-254.

Bibliography

1. Verginia Vedinas, *Mutații aduse în statutul funcționarilor publici prin O.U.G. nr. 37/2009,* in volume *Liber amicorum Nicolae Popa,* Hamangiu Publishing House, Bucharest, 2009, pp. 249-254.
2. Verginia Vedinaş, *Tratat teoretic şi practic de drept administrativ*, vol. I, Universul Juridic Publishing House, Bucharest, 2018.
3. Cătălin-Silviu Săraru, *Drept administrativ. Probleme fundamentale ale dreptului public*, C. H. Beck Publishing House, Bucharest, 2016.
4. Government Emergency Ordinance no. 57/2019 regarding the Administrative Code, published in the Official Gazette, Part I no. 555 of July 5, 2019, as amended.

LEGAL ASPECTS OF ELECTRONIC COMMUNICATION AND ITS REGULATION IN THE ADMINISTRATIVE PROCEDURE CODE

ASSOCIATE PROFESSOR MARGARITA CHESHMEDZHIEVA[1]

Abstract: *The entry into force of the amendments of the Administrative Procedure Code governing electronic communication lays out new challenges for citizens and administrative and legal authorities. The purpose of this article is to briefly present the results of an analysis of the new rules on announcing and summoning administrative proceedings, according to their regulation in the Administrative Procedure Code.*

Keywords: *electronic communication, announcing, summoning, e-justice, administrative law, Administrative Procedure Code.*

JEL Classification: K23

1. Introductory considerations

In the autumn of 2018, Bulgaria's basic administrative procedural law underwent significant changes, affecting a number of areas and changing traditional views on the regulation of administrative matters. The most important areas affected by the changes to the Administrative Procedure Code (APC)[2] relate to e-justice; the procedure for sending messages and summonses; the procedure in which interested parties refer to

[1] Margarita Cheshmedzhieva, Department of Public Law, Faculty of Law and History, South-West University "Neofit Rilski", Blagoevgrad, Bulgaria, margo4@abv.bg.

[2]Administrative Procedure Code, prom.SG, issue. 30 of April 11, 2006, effective July 12, 2006, as amended and Suppl. 77 of 18 September 2018, effective January 1, 2019; ed. by Decision No. 5 of the Constitutional Court of the Republic of Bulgaria dated 19 April 2019, issue. 36 of 3 May, 2019.

a competent authority; issues of jurisdiction; and cassation proceedings.

The amendments to the Administrative Procedure Code significantly expanded the assumptions surrounding electronic communication, "for the first time settling the method of communication, common to all administrative proceedings, in particular the exchange of documents in administrative proceedings"[3]. This, in turn, poses serious challenges for citizens, as well as administrative and law enforcement authorities. The key areas of focus are the implementation of electronic technologies and use of their capabilities. Electronic messages should facilitate, not hinder, proceedings. The significance of the amendments to the APC is also confirmed by the fact that there are already a number of studies dedicated to new legislative decisions[4].

2. Electronic communication and its regulation in the Administrative Procedure Code

The amendments to the APC mean that claims; signals and proposals; complaints; protests; applications; and claims and annexes to them may be submitted to administrative bodies, judicial authorities, public officials and organizations providing public services by electronic means. In proceedings before administrative bodies, the procedure is regulated by the Electronic Governance Act (EGA), while in proceedings before a court it is regulated by the Judiciary Act[5]. Administrative bodies, judicial authorities, public officials and public service organizations are obliged to have the technical capacity to communicate electronically.

The legislature, taking into account that some participants are not able to make full use of the possibilities offered by e-government and electronic document exchange, has also retained the traditional ways of

---

[3] Тодоров, Иван, Кино Лазаров, *Административен процес, с измененията на АПК от септември 2018*, София, Сиела, 2018г., p. 83 (Todorov, Ivan, Cinema Lazarov, *Administrative process, with the amendments of the APC from September 2018*, Sofia, Ciela, 2018, p. 83).

[4] *Ibid.*, Сивков, Цветан, *Измененията на Административнопроцесуалния кодекс от есента на 2018г.*, София, Сиби, 2019г. (Sivkov, Tsvetan, *Amendments to the Administrative Procedure Code of the Autumn 2018*, Sofia, Sibi, 2019), Янкулова, Соня, Теодора Николова, *Промените в Административнопроцесуалния кодекс—2018*, София, ИК "Труд и право", 2018г (Yankulova, Sonia, Teodora Nikolova, *Changes in the Administrative Procedure Code—2018*, Sofia, "Labor and Law" IC, 2018).

[5] Judiciary Act, promulgated SG. 64 of August 7, 2007, as amended and suppl., issue 29 of Apr. 8, 2019.

doing so, for example, by a licensed postal operator, as well as by fax or otherwise, and as published by such authorities on their websites. What is more, citizens can also submit their claims to administrative authorities orally, while organizations submit their claims in writing. The oral submission of claims to judicial authorities is inadmissible, as the provision of Art. 150 para. 1 of the APC explicitly requires a complaint to be in written form, as well as having certain content.

According to the provision of Art. 29 para. 2 of the APC, when an application for the initiation of administrative proceedings is made in writing, a signature is mandatory, as well as identification by name and address. Therefore, where the application is made electronically, as an electronic message, it should be signed and contain a qualified electronic signature. According to Art. 25, item 2 of Regulation (EU) No. 910/2014[6], the legal force of a qualified electronic signature is equivalent to that of a handwritten signature.

The filing of an application by an interested party starts administrative proceedings, which is why when submitting the application as an electronic message there must be evidence of the message being both sent and received. The APC provides for electronic communication with administrative bodies to be carried out in accordance with the procedure of the EGA. The activity of administrative bodies when working with electronic documents, the provision of administrative services by electronic means, and the exchange of electronic documents between administrative bodies is regulated by the Electronic Governance Act[7].

Administrative bodies, public officials, and public service organizations are all obliged to provide services within their competence electronically, unless the law provides for a particular form for performing particular actions or issuing relevant acts. Administrative bodies, public officials, and organizations providing public services are obliged to provide internal electronic administrative services in accordance with the EGA[8].

---

[6] Regulation (EU) No. 910/2014 of the European Parliament and of the Council of July 23, 2014 on electronic identification and trust services for electronic transactions in the internal market and repealing Directive 1999/93/EC.

[7] Electronic Governance Act, Prom. SG issue 46 of June 12, 2007, effective as of June 13, 2008, as amended and Suppl. 94 of November 13, 2018.

[8] EGA (Electronic Governance Act), Art. 39. (1) Internal electronic administrative services shall be internal administrative services, which may be requested and/or provided remotely by electronic means.

(2) Internal electronic administrative services shall also include services, which may be requested and/or provided remotely by electronic means, offered by the persons

Therefore, electronic communication in administrative proceedings, insofar as there is no explicit provision otherwise in the APC, is carried out in accordance with the EGA, which provides for the construction and maintenance of a unified access portal to electronic administrative services[9], an information system for safe service provision, and a qualified electronic registered mail service within the meaning of Regulation (EU) No. 910/2014.

In accordance with the requirements of the ordinance on the general requirements for information systems, registers, and electronic administrative services[10], the application is considered to have been received by the administrative body (the so-called "administrative service provider") at the time of its entry into its information system. Service of electronic statements by the providers of electronic administrative services may be carried out by sending a message to the electronic address containing information for downloading the final document from the secure service information system or from the unified portal. Documents are considered delivered upon their download.

The electronic delivery of documents can be certified with a copy of the electronic record of sending or downloading, and such documents are stored in a secure service information system or in the unified portal. The service may also be certified by a qualified e-mail service provider within the meaning of Regulation (EU) No. 910/2014[11]. If the recipient has not downloaded the document within seven days of its sending, the document shall be returned in the order determined by law, i.e. according to the procedure provided in the APC and not in cases dealing with electronic communication.

We fully support Prof. Todorov's opinion that the rules as regulated in the EGA do not correspond to the provisions of the APC and

---

charged with public functions and by the organisations providing public services, between each other, as well as to administrative bodies.

(3) Internal electronic administrative services may also be provided by administrative bodies to persons charged with public functions and to organisations providing public services.

[9] The unified access portal to electronic administrative services provides information on all electronic administrative services of all administrative bodies, persons performing public functions and organizations providing public services, as well as linking to an electronic form for their application.

[10] Ordinance on the General Requirements for information systems, registers and electronic administrative services, in force as of March 1, 2017, adopted by CoM Decree No. 3 of January 1, 2017, prom. SG. Issue 5 of January 17, 2017, amend. SG. issue 66 of 10 August 2018.

[11] Art. 26, para. 4 of the EGA.

the relevant provisions should be amended[12]. For example, in Art. 57 para. 2 of the APC it is provided that administrative acts under Art. 21 paras. 2 and 3 shall be issued within seven days of the date of the opening of proceedings. If during the proceedings the administrative authority sends an e-mail to a party in the proceedings, it should wait seven days to see whether the recipient will access it and in this case the time limit for issuing the administrative act is likely to have expired. In the provision of Art. 41 paras. 1 and 2, three days are provided for certain actions to be taken and if, again, the authority has to wait seven days to see if the message has been downloaded, then these deadlines cannot be met. It is precisely because of future amendments to the laws that these flaws should be corrected and the deadlines synchronized.

The provision of Art. 18a para. 3 regulates the filing of a complaint or protest electronically. This is done through the body that issued the disputed act under the Electronic Governance Act. Within three days of the expiry of the deadline for appealing by other persons, the authority shall send the complaint or protest to the court together with a certified copy of the entire file on the issue of the action, informing the sender thereof. If the authority fails to fulfill its obligation, a copy of the complaint or protest may be filed electronically with the court pursuant to the Judiciary Act, and the court then requests an official copy from the authority that issued the action. In our view, the legislation is inaccurate, since it is not clear whether the certified copy will be made electronically or on paper. In practice, a certified copy means a paper document. The filing of a copy of the complaint or protest to the court is not regulated in sufficient detail. Therefore, we agree with Prof. Sivkov that this provision should be improved[13].

The provision of Art. 18a, para. 5 of the APC assigns duties to administrative bodies; the judicial authority; public officials and organizations providing public services; organizations and lawyers; and participants in proceedings. They must specify an e-mail address under the Electronic Governance Act in proceedings before an administrative body or an e-mail address under the Judiciary Act in proceedings before a court for summoning and receiving documents and messages. Therefore, they also have an additional obligation to regularly check for messages received in this way.

On the other hand, the participation of citizens through electronic communication is a right and depends on their access to relevant technologies and their willingness to use them. Unlike administrative

---

[12] Тодоров, Иван, Кино Лазаров, (Todorov, Ivan, Cinema Lazarov), *op. cit.*, p. 91.

[13] София, Сиби, (Sivkov, Tsvetan), *op. cit.* p. 20.

authorities and their equivalents, the applicant or complainant, as well as all interested citizens who have been attracted or are seeking to intervene, in summoning and receiving documents and messages related to such proceedings, provide the administrative authority or the court with information, if they have a personal account registered in the secure electronic information system, an e-mail for receiving messages, a mobile or landline phone number, or a fax number, i.e. this is a matter of decision and wish, not of obligation.

If the message cannot be delivered electronically, traditional means can be used to do so, such as oral notification, by service at the address indicated by the party. If the party cannot be found at the address, communication can be undertaken by gluing a notification to a door or a mailbox. The final option is to place the message on the notice board or website of the relevant authority.

The APC also provides for changes in court proceedings regarding communications and summonses. Electronic communication in court proceedings is carried out through the Unified e-Justice Portal, according to the Judiciary Act. The rules for reporting in the EGA and Judiciary Act are generally the same and should meet the requirements for a qualified electronic registered mail service. The provision of Art. 137 of the APC provides that communications related to court proceedings shall be made in compliance with the rules for communication generally in administrative proceedings.

3. Conclusions

In conclusion, we can say that the aim of these innovations is to create a common procedure to which the acts and actions of all parties involved in administrative and judicial proceedings should be subject. This is a significant step forward in the introduction and use of electronic documents, the electronic identification of persons, and the administration and exchange of electronic messages, which, in turn, will lead to better facilitated procedural actions and an increase in the speed of service provision and greater convenience for recipients.

Bibliography

1. Тодоров, Иван, Кино Лазаров, *Административен процес, с измененията на АПК от септември 2018*, София, Сиела, 2018г (Todorov, Ivan, Cinema Lazarov, *Administrative process, with the amendments of the APC from September 2018*, Sofia, Ciela, 2018).

2. Сивков, Цветан, *Измененията на Административнопроцесуалния кодекс от есента на 2018г.*, София, Сиби, 2019г (Sivkov, Tsvetan, *Amendments to the Administrative Procedure Code of the Autumn 2018*, Sofia, Sibi, 2019).
3. Янкулова, Соня, Теодора Николова, *Промените в Административнопроцесуалния кодекс—2018*, София, ИК “Труд и право”, 2018г (Yankulova, Sonia, Teodora Nikolova, *Changes in the Administrative Procedure Code—2018*, Sofia, “Labor and Law” IC, 2018).
4. Regulation (EU) No. 910/2014 of the European Parliament and of the Council of July 23, 2014 on electronic identification and trust services for electronic transactions in the internal market and repealing Directive 1999/93/EC.
5. Electronic Governance Act, Prom. SG issue 46 of June 12, 2007, effective as of June 13, 2008, as amended and Suppl. 94 of November 13, 2018.
6. Administrative Procedure Code, prom.SG, issue. 30 of April 11, 2006, effective July 12, 2006, as amended and Suppl. 77 of 18 September 2018, effective January 1, 2019; ed. by Decision No. 5 of the Constitutional Court of the Republic of Bulgaria dated 19 April 2019, issue. 36 of 3 May, 2019.
7. Ordinance on the General Requirements for information systems, registers and electronic administrative services, in force as of March 1, 2017, adopted by CoM Decree No. 3 of January 1, 2017, prom. SG. Issue 5 of January 17, 2017, amend. SG. issue 66 of 10 August 2018.

PART III.

CONTEMPORARY CHALLENGES IN EUROPEAN AND COMPARATIVE ADMINISTRATIVE LAW

THE PRINCIPLE OF REVOCATION IN ROMANIAN ADMINISTRATIVE LAW: THE EXCEPTION REGARDING ADMINISTRATIVE ACTS THAT HAVE ENTERED THE CIVIL CIRCUIT AND PRODUCED LEGAL EFFECTS

PHD STUDENT
NICOLAE-ALEXANDRU CESLEA[1]

Abstract: *In administrative law, private law gains autonomy when a civil legal relationship is born. Regarding the specific terminology of administrative law, this legal phenomenon takes the form of the exception from the principle of revocation by an administration of administrative acts that have entered the civil circuit and produced legal effects. This paper addresses the issue of the moment up to the point when it is considered that an administrative act has entered the civil circuit and produced legal effects, keeping in mind that, in establishing the concepts with which the exception operates, an important role is played by traditional law and the historical evolution of legal norms. At the same time, analysis of the current doctrine and relevant case law are effective in outlining the applicable legal regime, as well as for identifying regulatory inconsistencies. The moment by which an administrative act can be revoked is essential, as certain projects can be stopped by the administration itself. In this context, the business environment does not just revolve around the conclusion of contracts, but also covers a number of important material acts prior to their conclusion, including the contribution of valuable material and human resources. At the civil procedure level, the incidence of the analyzed exception entails obligation or exemption from following the administrative*

[1] Nicolae-Alexandru Ceslea, Doctoral School of Law Faculty, University of Bucharest, Romania, alex.ceslea@ymail.com.

procedure before administration—an aspect that often raises issues regarding the principle of free access to justice.

***Keywords**: administrative act, administration, civil legal relationship, revocation, exception, civil circuit.*

JEL Classification: K23

1. Introduction

The principle of revocation of an administrative act and the exceptions to this principle concern the functioning of an administration and determine its prerogatives in relation to the means by which it acts.

Administrative law tends to penetrate all aspects of legal life and, against the background of the development of society, the business environment find itself confronted more and more with the institutions of this branch of law.

One of the forms in which administrative law makes its presence felt in the business environment is precisely at the level of the relationship between the administrative act and civil legal relationships; it gravitates around the moment up to the point when a public authority can revoke an administrative act.

This paper addresses those problems raised by the limits on the right to revoke an administrative act by an administration—this is the field of applying the exception to the principle of revocation of administrative acts that have entered the civil circuit and produced legal effects. The salient points regarding the conditions in which an administrative act becomes irrevocable are analyzed, being those up to the moment when it is considered that an administrative act can no longer be revoked.

In establishing the concepts with which the exception operates and its mechanism, it is important to use the historical-evolutionary method of research, considering that the regulation of contemporary administrative law has its origins in traditional administrative law.

Methods of interpretation, being grammatical and systematic, tend to extend the scope of the exception in question and offer different solutions to the evolutionary approach. This approach allows us to make the observation that the exception was taken from traditional law, but also allows us to observe the reasons that form the basis of regulating the exception in question.

This study also highlights a number of practical cases concerning the legal regime of the revocation of administrative acts and draws attention to the need for prudent behaviour by participants in the business environment. Behind every civil legal relationship we find an administrative legal act—ignoring this fact or using a too relaxed interpretation of public law rules can generate disputes leading to the failure of important projects or even the loss of a developer's credibility and the failure of their business.

This paper is divided into five sections. The first section conceptualizes the principle of revocation; sections 2 to 4 concern the exception to the principle of revocation of administrative acts that have entered the civil circuit and produced legal effects, dealing with topics such as the genesis of the exception, the context of the adoption of Law no. 554/2004[2] regarding administrative appeals, and the modifications of the legal regime subsequent to Law no. 554/2004 in relation to the exception, thus following its evolutionary path. Finally, in section 5, a series of issues regarding the purpose of the current regulation and the way in which the exception operates are raised.

2. The principle of revocation[3]

The legal doctrine defines the revocation of an administrative act as "*a way of totally or partially terminating the effects of a legal act, which is attracted by certain vices of the illegality or non-opportunity of an administrative act*"[4]. A revocation is regarded as a legal operation by which an administrative act is terminated or, as the case may be abrogated or even withdrawn, by its issuing body or a higher body in the administrative hierarchy; by its own motion or at the request of a person concerned[5].

---

[2] Law no. 554/02 December 2004 regarding administrative appeals, published in the Official Journal of Romania, Part I, no. 1154/07 December 2004.

[3] This paper is an adaptation of research carried out within the program of the doctoral law school of the Faculty of Law, University of Bucharest, presented in Research Report no. 1 and defended on September 30, 2019 (unpublished), before a commission composed of coordinator Prof. Univ. Dr. Verginia Vedinaș, Assoc. Univ. Dr. Dan Drosu Șaguna, Assoc. Univ. Dr. Alexandru-Sorin Ciobanu and Lecturer Univ. Dr. Bogdan Dima.

[4] Verginia Vedinaș, *Tratat teoretic şi practic de drept administrativ*, vol. II, Juridical Universe Publishing House, Bucharest, 2018, p.93.

[5] Cătălin-Silviu Săraru, *Drept administrativ. Probleme fundamentale ale dreptului public*, C. H. Beck Publishing House, Bucharest, 2016, p. 105-109; Lucian Chiriac, *Drept administrativ. Activitatea autorității administrației publice*, Hamangiu Publishing House, Bucharest, 2011, p.150; Alexandru-Sorin Ciobanu, *Drept administrativ. Activitatea administrației publice. Domeniul Public*, Universal Juridic Publishing House, Bucharest, 2015, p.91; Antonie Iorgovan, *Tratat de drept administrativ*, Vol. II, 4th edition, All Beck Publishing House, Bucharest, 2005, p.

Regarding administrative contracts[6], it is not a question of revocation[7], but of terminating the effects of an administrative contract through the will of the contracting parties[8]. Revocation is, however, a unilateral administrative act[9] that cannot overcome the manifestation of the will of the other party, as a legally valid contract involves a meeting of the minds[10]. At most, it may be considered that the intention to extinguish a legal relationship born of a contract takes the form of an act of revocation by the administration, as an administrative act undertaken at the request of a contractor, while the assimilated administrative act, being the contract, ceases only with the concord of the contracting parties.

The concept of revocation is a traditional concept in administrative law. It has not undergone significant changes during the period between the emergence of administrative law, based on the principle of the proper separation of powers, and the present moment. As a direct consequence of

---

83; Rodica Narcisa Petrescu, *Drept administrativ*, Hamangiu Publishing House, Bucharest, 2009, p. 346; Ovidiu Podaru, *Drept administrativ. Vol. I. Actul administrativ. (I) Repere pentru o teorie altfel*, Hamangiu Publishing House, Bucharest, 2010, p. 282; Verginia Vedinaș, *op. cit.*, vol. II, p. 93.

[6] Assimilated administrative acts within the meaning given by art. 2 paragraph (1) letter c) ind. 1 of Law no. 554/2004. According to this legal text, they: "*are assimilated to the administrative acts, within the meaning of the present law, the contracts concluded by public authorities that have as an object the valuation of public property, the execution of works of public interest, the provision of public services, and public procurement; by special laws, other categories of administrative contracts can be provided*".

[7] The pre-trial administrative complaint procedure regulated by art. 7 paragraph (6) of Law no. 554/2004 refers to reasons for the cancellation of a contract and so it does not concern other causes that cease the effects of the contract, such as unilateral termination, or specific termination in common law, and even unilateral modification of the contract. For details, see Alexandru-Sorin Ciobanu, *op. cit.*, pp. 129-131; Antonie Iorgovan, *op. cit.*, vol. II, p. 118, Verginia Vedinaș, *op. cit.*, vol. II, pp. 115-116.

[8] On the termination of the effects of the administrative contract see Cătălin-Silviu Săraru, *Contractele administrative. Reglementare, doctrină, jurisprudență*, C. H. Beck Publishing House, Bucharest, 2009, p. 304-315.

[9] In the inter-war doctrine, it was also held that revocation implied the possibility of unilaterally abolishing an administrative act. In this respect see Constantin G. Rarincescu, *Contenciosul administrativ român*, 2nd edition, Alcalay & Co. Universal Publishing House, Bucharest, 1936, p. 118.

[10] Within the meaning of art. 1166 of the Civil Code, Law no. 287/17 July 2009 on the Civil Code, published in the Official Journal of Romania, Part I, no. 505/15 July 2011, a contract involves "*the agreement of wills between two or more persons with the intention of establishing, modifying or extinguishing a legal relationship*".

this, in general, assessments made at different doctrinal periods of administrative law remain fully valid.

Regarding the substantiation of the right of revocation, in the general theory of law, under the principle of the autonomy of will the possibility of a legal subject to withdraw an act issued by it is recognized and revocation finds justification in this possibility[11].

Revocation goes to the essence of administration and the autonomy of an administration in carrying out its activities. From the interwar period on, the prerogative of an authority to exercise its right of administration, to freely overturn administrative acts and operations, and to control hierarchically inferior authorities has been recognized[12].

The principle of the autonomy of an administrative authority lies in "*its task to take the necessary measures to ensure the fulfillment of the needs of social life and the functioning of public services meant to satisfy these needs, in continuous and eternal change. That is why it must have the power at all times to take the necessary measures, either by developing new ones or by abolishing the old ones, which no longer correspond to new situations*"[13]. From this point of view, the problem arises in terms of legality and opportunity, and the act of an administrative authority being at all times revocable and enforceable by itself.

Revocation should also be considered in relation to the idea that an administration can adapt to social reality, being able to reconsider its position in terms of the evolution of society[14]. An administration can reconsider its position even when a change in perspective regarding the correspondence between the existing solution and the public interest occurs.

The principle of the revocation of administrative acts was imposed as a principle determined by the specific activity of the administration tied to the effective application of the law. It was recognized in the doctrine of the post-war period, although there was no text regulating this principle[15].

Currently, revocation relies on the provisions of art. 52[16] of the

---

[11] Ovidiu Podaru, *op. cit.*, p. 281, in which the theory of P. Salvatore, *Revoca degli atti administrazioni (III)*, in the Enciclopedia Giuridica (Treccani), vol. XXVII, Rome, 1991, p. 1 is highlighted.

[12] Constantin G. Rarincescu, *op. cit.*, p. 118.

[13] *Ibid.*

[14] Dumitru Brezoianu, Mariana Oprican, *Administrația publică în Romania*, C. H. Beck Publishing House, Bucharest, 2008, pp. 90-94.

[15] Antonie Iorgovan, *op. cit.*, vol. II, p. 83; Rodica Narcisa Petrescu, *op. cit.*, p. 346.

[16] According to these legal provisions: "*The person harmed in his right or in a legitimate interest, by a public authority, by an administrative act or by not resolving within the legal term of an application, is entitled to obtain recognition of the*

constitution and on the letter and spirit of Law no. 554/2004. At the same time, it has been held that if a court can annul an administrative act, so an administration can revoke it[17]. However, it is not just the fact that the court can terminate the administrative act—the controlling body or a hierarchically superior body can also cancel it within the administrative remedies regulated by law.

In fact, the principle of revocation has its source in the attributes conferred onto an administration in the prerogative of executing the provisions contained in law and ensuring the good functioning of administrative services. The administrative hierarchy thus formed presupposes the delegation of attributions, precisely implying the exercise of prerogatives conferred on the executive, and other attributes conferred by the doctrine onto the administrative body that refer to its functioning.

This opinion is also supported by the doctrine, which emphasizes, on the one hand, that the regime of public power evokes all the prerogatives granted to an administrative body by law, in order to promote the general interest[18]. This targets the organization, responsibility, procedure, and control of administrative acts, etc.[19]. On the other hand, it emphasizes that the regime of public power implies the derogative and explicit character of administrative law when compared to common law[20].

In this perspective an interesting parallel can be made between administrative law, in which the principle of the revocability of administrative acts originating in the regime of public power is recognized, and private law, with the principle of irrevocability of unilateral civil legal acts originating in the principle of compulsory force, which leads the author to conclude that limiting the principle of revocability in public law leads to

---

claimed right or the legitimate interest, annulment of the act and reparation of the damage". Moreover, it can be observed that the text does not show the ways available to the interested person to carry out his interest, which can be followed both before the court, but also before the administrative authority.

[17] Alexandru-Sorin Ciobanu, *op. cit.*, p. 92; Antonie Iorgovan, *op. cit.*, vol. II, p. 83.

[18] Antonie Iorgovan, *op. cit.*, vol.1, pp. 83-86, Rodica Narcisa Petrescu, *op. cit.*, p. 38, Verginia Vedinaş, *op. cit.*, vol.1, p. 54.

[19] Antonie Iorgovan, *op. cit.*, vol. I, p. 37.

[20] Ion Brad, *Revocarea actelor administrative. Instituţia revocării sub exigenţele dreptului European*, Universul Juridic Publishing House, Bucharest, 2009, p. 21. The author systematizes the prerogatives of the administration and divides them into privileges specific to the activity of the administration, namely the privilege of adopting administrative acts unilaterally, of the obligatory force of the administrative act, of the *ex officio* action, the privilege of solving cases by specialized courts, and, finally, the privilege of revocability. For details, see Ion Brad, *op. cit.*, pp. 32-44.

its approximation to private law[21].

Under the conditions of art. 1 paragraph (6)[22] of Law no. 554/2004, if the administrative act has entered the civil circuit and produced legal effects, then the principle of revocation no longer operates, implying that an authority can no longer terminate the effects of the administrative act that was the basis for the conclusion of a civil legal relationship.

Two distinct and cumulative conditions must be met so that an administrative act can no longer be revoked by an administrative body: the act has to produce legal effects and the act has to enter the civil circuit.

3. The genesis of the exception of the principle of revocation of administrative acts that have already entered the civil circuit and produced legal effects. The context of the adoption of Law no. 554/2004 regarding administrative appeals

Starting with the interwar period, the concept of an administrative act providing a basis for a civil contract was included in the category of exceptions to the principle of revocation. The reason for restricting the power of an administrative body to revoke an administrative act that, in the end, would also have resulted in the cancellation of a subsequent civil act, lay in avoiding the influence of administrative authority over private law relationships, as well as being a way of protecting their stability[23].

In the period after 1948, the exception was outlined as relating to administrative acts on the basis of which a contractual relationship was born and provided that both contracting parties were not subordinate to a hierarchically superior authority issuing the administrative act. The exception was justified by the way in which a contractual relationship arises, being based on the will of the parties, so that it cannot be abolished on the basis of the unilateral will of the issuer of the administrative act[24]. In other words, the way in which the two categories of legal relationship are formed, in administrative and private law, entailed the impossibility of modifying a bilateral act, a civil contract, by a unilateral act, being the administrative act.

The exception is applicable where a contract has been concluded

---

[21] *Ibid.*, pp. 40-44.

[22] According to art. 1 paragraph (6) of Law no. 554/2004: "*the act can no longer be revoked as it has entered the civil circuit and produced legal effects*".

[23] Constantin G. Rarincescu, *op. cit.*, pp. 121-122.

[24] Tudor Drăganu, *Actele de drept administrativ*, Scientific Publishing House, Bucharest, 1959, pp. 215, 234 and 238.

on the basis of an administrative act and where the contract was concluded to obtain an authorization. The reason for the exception also lies in protecting the stability of contracts and for reasons related to fairness, considering that an authority acts with the intention of facilitating the conclusion of civil legal relationships, or, as the case may be, in the context of their conclusion[25].

If the basic act was issued by an administrative body positioned above the contracting administrative bodies in the hierarchy, the will of the issuing administrative body will have to be fulfilled by the termination of the contract[26].

At the level of jurisprudence, Supreme Court decision no. 173/27 January 1956[27], after announcing the principle of the revocability of administrative acts, showed that once a civil legal relationship duplicates an administrative act, the administrative act becomes irrevocable.

From an analysis of the presented elements, it appears that in traditional administrative law an authority could not overturn its own measure or one adopted by a hierarchically inferior body after the moment when a civil legal relationship was born, in particular, when a contract was concluded on the basis or in the context of issuing the administrative act.

The exception to the principle of revocation was regulated for the first time by Law no. 554/2004 regarding administrative appeals. According to the statement justifying the legislative proposal[28] providing the content of Law no. 554/2004, the provision of art. 1 paragraph (7) of the project[29] "*regulates the right of the authority to request the cancellation of administrative documents that have entered the civil circuit*"[30].

---

[25] *Ibid.*, p. 218.
[26] *Ibid.*, p. 217.
[27] Decision no. 173/27 January 1956, pronounced by the Supreme Court, col. civ., in the "Legalitatea Populară" Review no. 5/1956, Journal of the Ministry of Justice, the General Prosecutor's Office and the Supreme Court of the People's Republic of Romania, pp. 614-615. Specifically, it analyzed the situation of a distribution order based on which a labour law relationship was concluded.
[28] In the draft law registered at the Chamber of Deputies under no. 243/28.06.2004, available on www.cdep.ro, last accessed 30.10.2019.
[29] According to this text: "*The public authority issuing the unlawful administrative act may request the annulment of its act in case the act, having entered the civil circuit and producing effects in other areas of law, can no longer be revoked*".
[30] Antonie Iorgovan, *Noua lege a contenciosului administrativ. Geneză şi explicaţii*, Roata Publishing House, Bucharest, 2004, p. 26.

The Legislative Council, regarding the legislative proposal entitled the Law of Administrative Appeals[31], proposed that: "*The public authority issuing the illegal administrative act can request the invalidation of its act in the case when the act can no longer be revoked, as it had entered the civil circuit and produced legal effects*"[32].

During the consultation pursued by the initiator of the project, the Timişoara Court of Appeal suggested the elimination of the text that became art. 1 paragraph (6), as quoted, claiming that the authority will invokes its own guilt in issuing the administrative document, and, in any case, after entering the civil circuit, against the multitude of legal effects that the administrative act can generate in society, it can limit the possibility of cancelling an administrative act[33].

In response to the observations received regarding the project, it was appreciated not only that the solution contained in the project was appropriate, but that it was also useful to insert a provision regarding the extension of the jurisdiction of the court to decide on civil acts concluded on the basis of administrative acts, the text being added accordingly[34]. Motivated by the need to clarify the situation surrounding civil acts concluded on the basis of an illegal administrative act, the observation became an amendment to the draft law[35].

---

[31] Address no. PLX 444/30.06.2004 submitted by the General Secretariat of the Chamber of Deputies, in Antonie Iorgovan, *Noua lege... op. cit.*, 2004, p. 40.

[32] Perhaps the wording of the legal provisions should have been correlated to the whole regulation, in order to avoid possible confusion, with the use of the formulation "*the administrative act considered illegal*", as happened in art. 1 paragraphs (1) and (2), art. 7 paragraphs (1) and (3) of Law no. 554/2004. Confusion could also generate the different terminology of art. 1 paragraph (6) and art. 7 paragraph (5) of the law, the first text referring to illegal administrative acts, while the latter does not distinguish between the legal or illegal character of the act, being able to appreciate in the sense that there is a difference of legal regime arising from the corroboration of these legal texts regarding the ability of an administration to revoke its own acts. However, the issue of legality or illegality is an element that is not determined from the beginning of the process when the problem of following the pre-trial administrative complaint procedure is also raised.

[33] Antonie Iorgovan, *Noua lege... op. cit.*, 2004, p. 85.

[34] According to this text: "*In case of admitting the action the court will decide, upon request, on the legality of civil acts concluded on the basis of an illegal administrative act, as well as on the civil effects produced*".

[35] Antonie Iorgovan, *Noua lege... op. cit.*, 2004, p. 120. The legal provisions were adopted in the following form: "*The issuing public authority of an illegal administrative act may request the court to ascertain its invalidity, in case the act can no longer be revoked, as it had entered the civil circuit and produced legal effects. In the case of admitting the action, the court will decide, upon request, also*

It was specified[36] that the regulation of this exception to the principle of revocability had as its purpose the elimination of disputes arising in jurisprudence regarding this case of revocation. Thus, for example, the case law prior to Law no. 554/2004 was somewhat similar to that enshrined in the doctrine, considering that: "*The principle of irrevocability of executed administrative acts or of those that have produced legal effects in other fields, leaving the exclusive regulatory sphere of administrative law, is a principle of general applicability. By enshrining this principle, the possibility of an administrative body reverting an issued administrative act is limited. An administrative act can be revoked, either for reasons of illegality or lack of opportunity, only until the administrative act has produced its effects by execution or by entry into the circuit of other legal relationships*"[37]. It is notable that the Supreme Court was even more restrictive in certain cases in the application of the exception than the one adopted by the traditional doctrine[38], in the sense that it was sufficient to execute the administrative act to make the act irrevocable.

On the other hand, contrary to this practice, it was held that "*even in the case where the contested administrative act has entered the civil circuit, as the first court argues, it is not possible to remove the obligation to perform this procedure* [the pre-trial administrative complaints procedure, i.e. the procedure in which the revocation of an administrative act is requested, o.n.]. *Regarding the eventual unconstitutional nature of the special legal provisions regarding the obligation of the prior administrative procedure, with reference to the administrative acts that have entered the civil circuit, the only competence to rule is that of the Constitutional Court, and not this court*"[39].

---

on the legality of the civil acts concluded on the basis of the illegal administrative act, as well as on the civil effects produced".

[36] Antonie Iorgovan, *Noua lege... op. cit.*, 2004, pp. 272-273.

[37] See decision no. 315/05 May 1994, delivered by the Supreme Court of Justice in Constantin Crişu, Nicorina Crişu Magraon, *Repertoriu de jurisprudenţă şi doctrină română: 1989-1994*, vol. II, Argessis Publishing House, Curtea de Argeş, 1994, p. 42.

[38] An opinion that tends to reappear also in the actual doctrine on the background of the new legislative changes. In this regard, see Cristian Clipa, *Ne îndreptăm spre facultativitatea plângerii administrative prealabile? Câteva observaţii pe marginea modificării neriguroase a art. 7 alin. (5) din Legea cu nr. 554/2004 a contenciosului administrativ*, from 01.10.2018, available on www.juridice.ro, last accessed 30.10.2019.

[39] See decision no. 1040/21 February 2005, pronounced by the High Court of Cassation and Justice, Section of Administrative and Fiscal Appeals, presented in Gabriela Bogasiu, *Procedura prealabilă în contenciosul administrativ: practică*

If other causes of revocation are not regulated, but recognized in the doctrine[40], then it is reasonable to note that the purpose of art. 1 paragraph (6) of Law no. 554/2004 was to solve the problem of jurisprudence faced by the courts, in the sense of recognizing this particular case relating to the revocation of administrative acts, and, subsequently, determining the competence of the administrative court to rule on the effects of an administrative legal act. From another perspective, we should also note that the purpose of regulation was not to revolutionize the legal regime of the exception, but to formalize legally what had been recognized in the doctrine since the interwar period.

It should also be noted that the second thesis of the analyzed text, the one regarding the jurisdiction of the administrative court, cannot explain the purpose of adopting the first thesis, the one regarding the exception to the revocation principle, since the genesis of the texts took place in reverse, from the central problem found in the first thesis to the subsequent problem found in the second thesis. In other words, the provisions of art. 1 paragraph (6) of Law no. 554/2004 were not adopted in the context of clarifying the competence of the administrative court to rule on the effects of an illegal administrative act, but rather to solve the case of revocation in question, the problem of competence subsequently raised, at the moment when the administration can no longer revoke the administrative act.

On the other hand, if it was not clear from the formulations already used in the adopted legal text, this addition of the second thesis implies that there must be a concrete assessment of the effects produced by the administrative act, returning the duty to the administration and/or the court to analyze the circumstances of the legal dispute from case to case, being beyond the scope of the legal provisions receiving an abstract interpretation and ignoring the circumstances of the case. The text was not conceived, nor could it be interpreted, in a way that the administrative act could no longer be revoked if it has the vocation to produce legal effects.

---

judiciară, Hamangiu Publishing House, Bucharest, 2006, pp. 12-16, pronounced under the conditions of Law no. 29/1990.

[40] For details, see Antonie Iorgovan, *op. cit.*, vol. II, pp. 85-94.

4. The modifications of the legal regime on the exception of administrative acts that have entered the civil circuit and produced legal effects through Law no. 262/2007 regarding the modification and completion of the Law on Administrative Litigation no. 554/2004

Through Law no. 262/2007[41], the form of the text of art. 1 paragraph (6)[42] of Law no. 554/2005 was modified. The legal provisions took the following form: "*The public authority issuing a unilateral unlawful administrative act can request the court to annul it, in the case when the act can no longer be revoked as it has entered the civil circuit and produced legal effects. In the case of admitting an action, the court decides, if it has been notified by a request for legal action, and on the validity of legal acts concluded on the basis of the illegal administrative act, as well as on the legal effects produced by them. The action may be brought within one year of the date of issue of the act*".

The modification of the wording of the phrase "*civil effects*" in "*legal effects*"[43] did not seek to change the philosophy underlying this exception, but aimed to clarify the terminological details and the establishment of a term under which the authority can request the annulment of an administrative act in court. Moreover, the modification concerns the second thesis of the text, which cannot influence the first thesis, as shown[44].

As such, from the explanatory statement to the draft of the amending Law no. 554/2004, which materialized in the content of Law no. 262/2007, it appears that the purpose of promoting the initiative was based on the correlation of the texts with certain decisions of the Constitutional Court. It sought to modify the formulation of the text, as problems of

---

[41] Law no. 262/19 July 2007 regarding the modification and completion of the Law on administrative disputes no. 554/2004, published in the Official Journal of Romania, Part I, no. 510/30 July 2007.

[42] In its initial form: "*The public authority issuing an illegal administrative act may request the court to ascertain its invalidity, in the event that the act can no longer be revoked, as it has entered the civil circuit and produced legal effects. In the case of admitting the action, the court will decide, upon request, also on the legality of the civil acts concluded on the basis of the illegal administrative act, as well as on the civil effects produced*".

[43] Indeed, the legal circuit has a much wider sphere, which also includes the civil circuit, for details see Ovidiu Podaru, *Drept administrativ. Practică judiciară comentată. Vol. I. Actul administrativ. (II) Un secol de jurisprudenţă (1909-2009)*, Hamangiu Publishing House, Bucharest, 2010, p. 328.

[44] See above in Section 2 of this paper.

interpretation and application were raised due to the drafting mode, the academic language in the relevant monographs and university treaties used, rather than the traditional technical-legal language of the Civil Procedure Code of 1864. Most of the changes related to legislative technique, following a better correlation of the texts to avoid different interpretations and without substantive changes to art. 1 paragraph (6) regarding the exception to the principle of revocation and art. 7 of Law no. 554/2004 regarding the preliminary procedure, as well as the pre-trial administrative complaint procedure.

In the previous form of the text of art. 1 paragraph (6) of the law, there was no reference to the term within which the authority could file a motion to annul the illegal individual administrative act before the courts, so that, considering the interpretation given by the High Court of Cassation and Justice of the provisions of art. 1 paragraph (6) in the old form, which became an observation in the process of amending Law no. 554/2004, the term of one year in which the authority could request the cancellation of the issued administrative act was established[45].

The wording "*the authority may request the court to establish grounds of annulment*" has been modified as "*the issuing public authority (...) can request the court to annul it*" to ensure greater rigour in the terminology.

Moreover, in the legal literature, subsequent to the adoption of Law no. 262/2007, art. 1 paragraph (6) of Law no. 554/2004 is also viewed in terms of civil effects, the notion "*in the civil circuit*" being explained precisely from this perspective as "*(...) the act entered the civil circuit, meaning once it started to produce civil legal effects (...)*"[46].

From this point of view, the phrase "*entered the civil circuit*" has an autonomous sense in administrative law, and not in the sense of adapting the syntax to the administrative matter. It is the sense in which it assumes that the act has entered the general or administrative circuit.

Thereby, observing the evolution of art. 1 paragraph (6) of Law no. 554/2004, only in appearance do the terms "*entered the civil circuit*" and "*produced legal effects*" have the same content. In fact, they have been associated to emphasize the connection of the legal effects of the administrative act produced in the civil domain, in particular, to contractual matters. In other words, it is not enough for an act to be issued,

---

[45] Antonie Iorgovan, Liliana Vişan, Alexandru-Sorin Ciobanu, Diana Iuliana Pasăre, *Legea contenciosului administrativ (Legea nr. 554/2004), cu modificările şi completările la zi. Comentariu şi jurisprudenţă*, Universul Juridic Publishing House, Bucharest, 2008, pp. 41-42.

[46] *Ibid.*, p. 43.

communicated or executed to be considered as having produced legal effects[47], but it must also have provided a basis for the conclusion of a civil legal relationship.

We note that the reasons considered at the time of entry into force of Law no. 554/2004 and the interpretation of them are still valid today, the evolutionary and systematic interpretation of the legal provisions being sufficient to draw this conclusion.

A part of the doctrine[48] concerns an even more restrictive notion and, therefore, the domain of application of the exception. This is in the sense that: a) the administrative act must be individual; b) it creates a patrimonial effect; c) the right acquired by the act engaged a context of good faith, since fraud cannot create rights; d) the right acquired had already been transacted[49] and had been the subject of a civil legal act; and e) the existence of a connection was so close that the revocation of the first would cause the second to be abolished.

The more restrictive version of the domain of application of the exception arises from the combination of the second and fourth conditions [b] and [d], resulting in the administrative act producing a patrimonial effect and coming to bear upon a transactional good. This is justified by the notion of the civil circuit, which represents "*the totality of the legal acts through which the goods (viewed as patrimonial values) circulate from one person to another*"[50]. Thus, if the administration issues an administrative act recognizing a college degree for a person and the civil act concluded does not aim to trade on this quality, we are not subject to the exception[51].

In a preferable variant of the evolutionary interpretation, with a corresponding rationale underlying the theory, as well as the sufficiently general formulation of the legal provisions to include the described hypothesis, we assume that the latter example falls under the exception of the principle of revocation. This would appear naturally so, since, based on the theory of the patrimonial effect of the administrative act proposed, comparable situations would receive different solutions: on the one hand, that of an administrative act that has as its object a patrimonial right and, on the other hand, that of an administrative act that recognizes a non-

---

[47] For a number of examples to observe when an administrative act takes effect, see Cristian Clipa, *op. cit.*.

[48] Ovidiu Podaru, *Repere ... op. cit.*, p. 288.

[49] Also, more restrictive, in the sense that the notion of civil circuit is similar to the notion of trade, Ovidiu Podaru, *Un secol... op. cit.*, p. 327.

[50] *Ibid.*

[51] The relevance of the example for the business environment is that obtaining a diploma can be the basis for hiring or promoting personnel in a company.

patrimonial right. The example regarding the recognition of a college degree is somewhat similar to the hypothesis of trading on the patrimonial effects arising from a non-patrimonial right, a situation that, even more so, can be integrated into the category of the given example.

5. The modifications of the legal regime made by Law no. 212/2018 for amending and supplementing the Law on administrative disputes no. 554/2004 and other normative acts

In Law no. 212/2018[52], the wording corresponding to the exception to the revocation of administrative acts found in art. 1 paragraph (6)[53] of Law no. 554/2004 was introduced to the provisions of art. 7 paragraph (5)[54] of the same normative act[55].

This modification of the legal regime regarding the exception to administrative acts that have entered the civil circuit and produced legal effects and the preliminary procedure is clear.

According to the statement of reasons for amending Law no. 554/2004[56], the modification aimed to correct the significant differences in the volume of activity between administrative sections and other sections of the courts. At the same time, it aimed to reduce the time-limits for resolving cases by eliminating some steps from the regularization procedure and the filtering of appeals in administrative litigation, as well as correlating the legal provisions to the Constitutional Court's decisions on administrative litigation and civil procedure.

Regarding the preliminary procedure, taking into account the explanatory statement, as well as the form of the text, it can be seen, once again, that the legislature's intention was not to rethink or introduce new concepts, but simply to correlate the provisions of art. 1 paragraph (6) to

---

[52] Law no. 212/25 July 2018 for amending and adding to the Law on administrative disputes no. 554/2004 and other normative acts, published in the Official Journal of Romania, Part I, no. 658/30 July 2018.

[53] According to the text: "*the act can no longer be revoked once it has entered the civil circuit and produced legal effects*".

[54] According to the legal text: "*In the case of (...) actions against administrative acts that can no longer be revoked as they have entered the civil circuit and produced legal effects, (...) no prior complaint is compulsory*".

[55] We note that, under the conditions of art. 7, paragraph (1) of Law no. 554/2004, with the preliminary procedure, the administrative act is revoked.

[56] The project registered at the Chamber of Deputies under no. Pl-x no. 76/2018 became Law no. 212/2018, available on www.cdep.ro, last accessed 30.10.2019.

those of art. 7 paragraph (5) of Law no. 554/2004, a solution that was already found in the practice of the courts.

As such, in a case prior to this modification by Law no. 212/2018, it was held that there was no obligation for the applicants to follow any previous procedure, considering the corroboration found in the provisions of art. 1 paragraph (6) and art. 7 paragraph (1) of Law no. 554/2004. The reason that the previous procedure was regulated, namely the avoidance of the process through the ability of an authority to revoke its own act, was foregrounded and it was stated that "*the public authority can no longer revoke the act, so it would be unreasonable for the previous procedure to be mandatory*"[57].

The amendments made by Law no. 262/2007 saw the provisions of art. 7 paragraph (5) of the law completed with the hypothesis on administrative acts assimilated in the form of an unjustified refusal by or a lack of response from an administrative body, as well as regarding the exception of illegality. Although the legal text was clear[58], it can equally be argued that this legislative correlation to the exception of administrative acts that have already entered the civil circuit and produced legal effects sought the attention of courts who chose not to take into account the fact that, for an administrative act that can no longer be revoked, no prior complaint is necessary.

The notion regarding the entry into the civil circuit of an administrative act must be looked at, first of all, with reference to the moment when it first appeared in the legislation through the modification made by Law no. 212/2018, which simply took over the concept for the purpose of legislative correlation, and then viewed in the historical context from the moment Law no. 554/2004 was adopted, which was the intention of the legislature in adopting this regulation.

---

[57] In this regard, sentence no. 5454/19.09.2018 was pronounced by the Bucharest Tribunal, Second Section of Administrative and Fiscal Appeals, in a case having as its object the suspension of authorization for construction, made definitive by not exercising the appeal procedure, unpublished.

[58] The formulations from the explanatory statement of the draft of the amending Law no. 554/2004, a project that materialized in the content of Law no. 262/2007 and was registered at the Chamber of Deputies under no. Pl-x no. 1/2007, available on www.cdep.ro, last accessed 30.10.2019, leave no room for interpretation in the sense that the modification came in the context of sending a signal to courts who chose not to apply the provisions of the law: "*one can discuss this position of the administrative litigation courts, but it is certain that some interpretations are exaggerated, the courts adding to the law (...) Where is the character of ambiguity? The text is very clear, analysis of the legality of an administrative act is done at any time, which means that the date of issue is irrelevant*".

In the doctrine[59], the method of restrictive interpretation of the text had not been agreed upon, in the sense that once it produced legal effects the administrative act had already entered the civil circuit and so the provisions establishing the principle of revocation and the preliminary procedure would no longer find applicability. In disagreeing with this restrictive interpretation, we add that there is also the argument that the legal provisions must be interpreted in the sense of their effects, according to the Latin adage *actus interpretandus est potius ut valeat quam pereat*, and not in the sense of not applying them. In other words, there is no reason to keep these legal institutions in law if there is no intention to apply them.

At the same time, the traditional doctrine and legislative evolution of Romanian law would be denied in this, it having been 50 years since the preliminary procedure became mandatory[60] and more than 150 years since the process of administrative appeal was recognized, therefore recognizing an administration body's right to revoke administrative acts[61].

However, the restrictive interpretation of the text covering the exception does not reflect the natural course of development of administrative law. The evolution of administrative law must pursue a policy of putting the administration at the forefront, treating it as a partner in achieving society's objectives, streamlining administrative processes, regulating institutions, and diversifying legal remedies. Marginalization of and loss of confidence in an administration should be avoided. The elimination of an administration from the control of an administrative act would send such a message: whenever the interpretation of a legal provision would present even the smallest problem or involve the assuming of some

---

[59] Ion Brad, *op. cit.*, pp. 106-107; Ovidiu Podaru, *Repere ... op. cit.*, p. 291; Dragoş Cosmin Dragoş, *Legea contenciosului administrativ. Comentarii şi explicaţii*, second edition, All Beck Publishing House, Bucharest, 2009, p. 50. In opposition, Cristian Clipa, *op. cit.*

[60] The mandatory pre-trial procedure was regulated for the first time by Law no. 1/1967 as regards judgments made by the courts of claims by those harmed through illegal administrative acts, published in the Official Bulletin no. 67/07 December 1967.

[61] The first form by which an administrative appeal was regulated is found in the provisions of art. 26 of Law no. 167/1864 for the establishment of a state council on 11 February 1864, published in the Official Journal of Romania of January 11, 1864, according to which "*the complaints raised by individuals for the defense of their interests, in certain cases determined by law, can be addressed directly to the State Council if those individuals have previously complained to the respective Ministry and have not obtained a reply within 15 days from the date of receipt of the complaint. The State Council will enter directly into the examination of such complaints*".

responsibility by an administration, it would give up responsibility for its resolution to the courts.

In terms of the practice of the courts[62], the case of an investment where no work had been executed for about eight years was encountered, the only activity had involved minimal preliminary work carried out in relation to the viability of the land and the arrangement of the premises before starting construction. Not only could the public authority revoke this authorization, but the court also established that the legal provisions in the matter constituted a legal cause of losing validity, highlighting, once again, a favourable solution to revocation.

The condition regarding entry into the civil circuit implies that the conclusion of a civil legal relationship based on an administrative act, negotiations regarding the conclusion of a contract, and preparatory acts to an investment or to work being performed under a building permit do not prevent an authority from revoking an administrative act.

Taking the hypothetical example of a residential complex, another situation might relate to the conclusion of contracts for the sale of a future good[63] or the promise of sale[64]. The conclusion of such contracts turns them into irrevocable administrative acts, insofar as the issuance of a building authorization permit supported the conclusion of such contracts. As such, there is a dependent link between the administrative act and the civil legal relationship. If the contracts were concluded independently of the issuance

---

[62] In this regard, see sentence no. 8497/18 December 2018, pronounced by the Bucharest Tribunal, Second Section of Administrative and Fiscal Appeals, appeal in progress, unpublished. After about eight years from the first authorization, given the legislative modification regarding urbanism indicators in the area, the investor requested the extension of his building permit, following, according to the *tempus regit actum* principle, that the urban norms applicable to the construction would be those in force from the moment of first authorization. Although the public authority issued the extension, the court annulled it, holding that the provisions of art. 7 paragraphs (6) and (7) of Law no. 50/1991 regarding the authorization of the execution of construction work, published in the Official Journal of Romania, Part I, no. 933/13 October 2004, according to which the failure to start or finalize works within the deadlines established by the authorization leads to its loss of validity.

[63] According to art. 1658 para. (1) of the Civil Code: "*If the object of the sale constitutes a future good, the buyer acquires the property at the moment when the good is realized. As regards construction, the corresponding provisions regarding the land book are applicable*".

[64] According to art. 1669 para. (1) of the Civil Code: "*When one of the parties that has concluded a bilateral promise of sale refuses, unjustifiably, to conclude the promised contract, the other party may ask for a decision to take the place of the contract, if all the other conditions of validity are met*".

of a building permit, such a case being in the hypothesis of the civil contracts concluded prior to the issuance of an authorization, the administrative act does not become irrevocable. The two conditions of the exception analyzed assume two legal relationships conditioned one by the other. In the latter case, it is not just that the administrative act could not enter the civil circuit, but that it could not produce legal effects, since it was not issued at the time the contracts were concluded.

6. Aspects regarding the rationale of the current regulation and mechanism of the exception. The case of illegal administrative acts

An interesting issue raised in the doctrine[65] concerns the reason why, after entering the civil circuit, an administrative act is no longer revocable, but can still be annulled by the court. As such, the reasons for this cannot be found in the protection of good faith, legal certainty, or legitimate trust, nor in the guarantees offered by the procedure of the court. This leads us to the conclusion that the reason for which it is no longer revocable, but it can be overturned by the court, cannot be determined.

Indeed, whether it is revoked by an administrative body or is annulled by the court, it is only a matter of time until the administrative act is removed from the legal order, the same fate befalling subsequent acts, including civil ones. On the contrary, it is preferable to permit an administration to revoke an illegal administrative act from the perspective of protecting the security of legal relationships and the civil circuit, since the act will no longer be the basis for the conclusion of other legal relationships.

In the doctrine[66], it has also been shown that, if it is possible to annul an administrative act through the courts, at the request of an authority or even by a third party, it would also be possible for the issuing authority to revoke it, the decision of revocation also being a decision of annulment.

Also[67], a contract arises through the agreement of the parties to it and termination takes place under the same conditions. In the case of disagreement, a court will decide on the termination of the contract. Another solution would imply that the revocation of a legal act that has already

---

[65] Ovidiu Podaru, *Repere ... op. cit.*, p. 293.

[66] Dacian Cosmin Dragoş, *Drept administrativ*, second edition, Accent Publishing House, Cluj-Napoca, 2005, pp. 82 and 85.

[67] Cătălin-Silviu Săraru, *Contenciosul administrativ român*, C. H. Beck Publishing House, Bucharest, 2019, p. 110.

entered the civil circuit and produced legal effects would affect the principle of civil circuit security and the stability of legal relationships.

Regarding the opinions expressed in the doctrine, according to the preceding paragraphs, in formulating a response to the highlighted problem the traditional rationale for the exception from the principle of revocation, which lies in avoiding the unilateral intervention of an authority in civil legal relationships, must be taken into account. Furthermore, it should be acknowledged that the legal mechanism of revocation in the case of this exception is devoid of any legal basis; *in principle*, two legal wills (the contract) cannot be overturned by a single (administrative act) or, in other words, the principle of consensualism should not be subordinate to the free will of the administration.

Since the hypothesis only concerns legally issued acts, including when revocation is ordered for reasons of opportunity, the cancellation of a subsequent act does not intervene as a consequence of illegality, but as a consequence of the will of the administration.

In the case of an illegal administrative act, the situation is distinct. The annulment of a subsequent act intervenes as a consequence of the effects of the principle of nullity. In the latter hypothesis, the situation being similar to that of civil law, in applying the principle *resoluto iure dantis, resolvitur ius accipiendis*, the principle of annulment of a subsequent act following the annulment of an initial act is a consequence of the annulment, respectively *nemo plus iuris ad alium transferre potest, quam ipse habet or nemo dat quod non habet*[68].

To exemplify this similarity with civil law, if the object of the contractual legal relationship is a good, which, subsequently, is the subject of another contractual legal relationship, and the parties of the first contract choose to amicably declare the intervention of nullity[69], for whatever reason, within the limits of the exceptions of the principle *resoluto...*, the subsequent act should be annulled. The annulment of the subsequent act does not intervene as a result of the will of the parties to amicably declare

---

[68] Principles recognized by art. 1254 para. (2) of the Civil Code, which establishes the rule for the cancellation of subsequent acts; art. 1325 of the Civil Code, which extends the termination rule to contracts; and art. 1648 of the Civil Code regarding the effects on third parties. For details see Gabriel Boroi, Carla Alexandra Anghelescu, *Curs de drept civil. Partea generală*, second edition, revised and added, Hamangiu Publishing House, Bucharest, 2012, p. 280.

[69] According to art. 1246 para. (3) of the Civil Code "*Unless otherwise provided by law, the nullity of the contract can be ascertained or declared by the agreement of the parties*", so that the nullity attracts the applicability of the principle *resoluto...*, and not the will of the parties.

nullification, but as an effect of the nullification, regardless of how it intervenes. In administrative law, the subsequent act is also annulled as an effect of the principle of nullity, and not as a result of the simple will of the authority.

However, this comparison with civil law also highlights a shortcoming arising from the difference between the legal regimes of civil and administrative law. In civil law, the legal regime is coherent and the exceptions to the principle *resoluto...* are expressly regulated by law and concern the protection of good faith, security, and the stability of the civil circuit[70], even the courts being held by them in their decisions. In contrast, in administrative law only the public authority is held by the exceptions to the principle of revocation, but not the courts. As a consequence, courts are placed in a position to judge using general principles of law, without a framework governed by administrative law.

It has also been claimed[71] that acts that have already entered the civil circuit and produced legal effects can be revoked if they involved fraud by the beneficiaries, motivated by the fact that the revocation of an illegal administrative act, and not on the basis of non-opportunity, is justified by the protection of the public interest.

We consider that, if, for purposes of administrative fraud, the administrative act can be revoked, then it can also be revoked in a hypothetical scenario where there is no fraud, but the act is illegal, since the legality comes to the foreground. The reasons for which the acts entered the civil circuit and produced legal effects are irrevocable.

However, at the current legislative stage, we consider that, for both legal and illegal administrative acts, the exception from the principle of revocation finds its only reason in the necessity of avoiding the unilateral intervention of an authority into civil law relationships.

The security of the legal relationship and the principle of legitimate trust intervene even at the trial stage, being principles that the court should also take into account, as they concern the wider legal framework. It is true that the jurisprudence of the European courts has raised questions about the security of legal relationships and the principle of legitimate trust in relation to the measure of revocation ordered by European administrative

---

[70] For example, the acquirer of a movable good who acts in good faith [art. 937 para. (1) of the Civil Code], even immovable property [art. 909 para. (3) and art. 908 para. (1) point 1 of the Civil Code], in relation to these exceptions the courts are also held in their decisions.

[71] Dacian Cosmin Dragoş, *Drept administrativ... op. cit.*, pp. 82 and 85.

authorities[72], but the issues raised have generally been specific to disputes regarding the civil service. Some contributions have looked at legal acts issued by European institutions and the legal regime of revocation and cancellation at European level. Finally, in terms of the specificity of domestic law and the legal regime, these should not be exactly applicable. The principles of the security of legal relationships and of legitimate confidence do not fall within the scope of the regulation of the analyzed exception and, as an effect of their application, it may be possible, under certain conditions, to remove the entire legal regime of the exception. This, however, is not the subject of the paper.

7. Conclusions

The exceptions to the principle of revocation have developed since the interwar period and have generally remained intact, including the exception regarding administrative acts that have entered the civil circuit and produced legal effects. The legal regime of this exception has been outlined in the doctrine in various forms, without necessarily considering the reasons behind it.

The rationale behind the traditional conception of the exception to the principle of revocation, which has been maintained up to now, lies in avoiding the unilateral intervention of an authority in civil law relationships. Furthermore, the legal mechanism of revocation in the case of this exception is devoid of any legal basis, at least in principle, and not able to overcome the concord of two legal wills (the contract) through a single one (the administrative act).

From the point of view of the traditional doctrine and its historical evolution, two distinct and cumulative conditions must be met for an administrative act to no longer be revocable by an administrative authority. The first condition lies in the need for the act to be issued, communicated, or executed to produce legal effects (the condition that the administrative act has produced legal effects) and the second lies in the conclusion of a civil legal relationship, i.e. a contract (the condition that the act has entered the civil circuit).

The current regulation also requires that the legal provisions establishing the analyzed exception are interpreted in concrete terms, on a case-by-case basis, and not in the abstract, ignoring the specific circumstances of the legal situation. The text has not been so conceived, nor

---

[72] In this regard, Ion Brad, *op. cit.*, pp. 122-173; Ovidiu Podaru, *Repere... op. cit.*, pp. 296-304; Cătălin-Sivliu Săraru, *op. cit.*, 2019, pp. 111-112.

can it be interpreted, that an administrative act can no longer be revoked if it has the intention of producing legal effects or is likely to enter the civil circuit.

The exception regarding administrative acts that have already entered the civil circuit and produced legal effects developed in a period when administrative litigation was in its infancy and appeals were exceptional[73]. In the current period, with judicial litigation having been elevated to the level of principle, and when all the acts of an administration can be verified, this exception should be rethought, since it appears to lead to the unjustified prohibition of an authority revoking an administrative act in a context where it is only a matter of time until the court annuls the illegal administrative act.

On the other hand, analyzing the whole national regulation in the field of administrative remedies, in the case of special administrative jurisdictions[74], an authority may order the cancellation of the administrative act with retroactive effect, even if the administrative act has entered the civil circuit and produced legal effects. In the same way, the case of acts subject to administrative appeal as regulated by law[75] should not be omitted. These

---

[73] For details, see Rîciu Iuliana, *Procedura contenciosului administrativ. Aspecte teoretice şi repere jurisprudenţiale*, Hamangiu Publishing House, Bucharest, 2012, pp. 16-21.

[74] The general framework of special administrative jurisdictions is regulated by art. 6 of Law no. 554/2004.

[75] By way of example, see the appeals submitted against measures ordered by a decision of the Court of Accounts or contrary to the deadline set for carrying out some of these measures. As such, according to point 204 of the Decision of the plenary of the Court of Accounts no. 155/2014 for the approval of the regulation regarding the organization and conduct of the activities of the Court of Accounts, as well as the valorization of the documents resulting from these activities, published in the Official Journal of Romania, Part I, no. 547/24 July 2014: "*Against the measures ordered by the decision, as well as the deadline established for carrying out some of these measures, within 15 calendar days from the date of its receipt, the head of the verified entity may lodge/submit an appeal to the Court of Auditors that issued the decision. The appeal against the decision issued by the specialized structure of the Court of Accounts represents a mandatory pre-trial procedure to exercise the right of action in administrative litigation*". See also the request for a review of the rejection of registration or deletion in the land register addressed to the chief registrar within the territorial office. As such, according to art. 50 paragraph (2) of Law no. 7/1996 of the cadastre and real estate advertising, published in the Official Journal of Romania, Part I, no. 720/24 September 2015: "*The interested person or the notary public can file a request for a review of admission or rejection, within 15 days of communication, which is resolved within 20 days by the chief registrar of the territorial office within which the building is located*".

can only put in an unfavorable light the intention to widen the domain of the application of the analyzed exception, or even the legislature's intention to maintain limits on the right of revocation.

Bibliography

1. Alexandru-Sorin Ciobanu, *Drept administrativ. Activitatea administrației publice. Domeniul Public*, Universul Juridic Publishing House, Bucharest, 2015.
2. Antonie Iorgovan, Liliana Vişan, Alexandru-Sorin Ciobanu, Diana Iuliana Pasăre, *Legea contenciosului administrativ (Legea nr. 554/2004), cu modificările şi completările la zi. Comentariu şi jurisprudență*, Universul Juridic Publishing House, Bucharest, 2008.
3. Antonie Iorgovan, *Noua lege a contenciosului administrativ. Geneză şi explicații*, Roata Publishing House, Bucharest, 2004.
4. Antonie Iorgovan, *Tratat de drept administrativ*, Vol. I and II, 4th edition, All Beck Publishing House, Bucharest, 2005.
5. Brad Ion, *Revocarea actelor administrative. Instituția revocării sub exigențele dreptului european*, Universul Juridic Publishing House, Bucharest, 2009.
6. Cătălin-Silviu Săraru, *Contenciosul administrativ român*, C. H. Beck Publishing House, Bucharest, 2019.
7. Cătălin-Silviu Săraru, *Drept administrativ. Probleme fundamentale ale dreptului public*, C. H. Beck Publishing House, Bucharest, 2016.
8. Cătălin-Silviu Săraru, *Contractele administrative. Reglementare, doctrină, jurisprudență*, C. H. Beck Publishing House, Bucharest, 2009.
9. Constantin G. Rarincescu, *Contenciosul administrativ român*, second edition, Alcalay & Co. Universal Publishing House, Bucharest, 1936.
10. Cristian Clipa, *Ne îndreptăm spre facultativitatea plângerii administrative prealabile? Câteva observații pe marginea modificării neriguroase a art. 7 alin. (5) din Legea cu nr. 554/2004 a contenciosului administrativ*, from 01.10.2018, available on www.juridice.ro, last accessed 30.10.2019.
11. Crişu Constantin, Crişu Magraon Nicorina, *Repertoriu de jurisprudență şi doctrină română: 1989-1994*, vol. II, Argessis Publishing House, Curtea de Argeş, 1994.
12. Dacian Cosmin Dragoş, *Drept administrativ*, second edition, Accent Publishing House, Cluj-Napoca, 2005.
13. Dragoş Cosmin Dragoş, *Legea contenciosului administrativ.*

Comentarii şi explicaţii, second edition, All Beck Publishing House, Bucharest, 2009.

14. Dumitru Brezoianu, Mariana Oprican, *Administraţia publică în Romania*, C. H. Beck Publishing House, Bucharest, 2008.
15. Gabriel Boroi, Carla Alexandra Anghelescu, *Curs de drept civil. Partea generală*, second edition, revised and added, Hamangiu Publishing House, Bucharest, 2012.
16. Gabriela Bogasiu, *Procedura prealabilă în contenciosul administrativ: practică judiciară*, Hamangiu Publishing House, Bucharest, 2006.
17. Iuliana Rîciu, *Procedura contenciosului administrativ. Aspecte teoretice şi repere jurisprudenţiale*, Hamangiu Publishing House, Bucharest, 2012.
18. Lucian Chiriac, *Drept administrativ. Activitatea autorităţii administraţiei publice*, Hamangiu, Bucharest, 2011.
19. Ovidiu Podaru, *Drept administrativ. Practică judiciară comentată. Vol. I. Actul administrativ. (II) Un secol de jurisprudenţă (1909-2009)*, Hamangiu Publishing House, Bucharest, 2010.
20. Ovidiu Podaru, *Drept administrativ. Vol. I. Actul administrativ. (I) Repere pentru o teorie altfel*, Hamangiu Publishing House, Bucharest, 2010.
21. Rodica Narcisa Petrescu, *Drept administrativ*, Hamangiu Publishing House, Bucharest, 2009.
22. Verginia Vedinaş, *Tratat teoretic şi practic de drept administrativ*, vol. I and II, Universul Juridic Publishing House, Bucharest, 2018.

The Validity of a Tender Proposal and of the Participation Guarantee: Between the Will of the Contracting Authority and that of the Bidder. A Synthesis of the Relevant Case Law in Public Procurement

PhD. Cosmin SOARE-FILATOV[1]

Abstract: *Participation in a public procurement procedure represents the manifestation of an economic operator's will. In certain cases, however, this will may be limited by the contracting authority. This study looks into whether this sort of limitation may be brought by way of an instrument common to all tender procedures, namely the determination of the proposal's and the participation guarantee's period of validity. An analysis of the relevant case law reveals heterogeneous practices, where the literal interpretation of the law is in conflict with the spirit of the law.*

Keywords: *public procurement, public authority, validity, heterogeneous practice.*

JEL Classification: K12, K23

1. Justification of the study

The national strategy in the realm of public procurement for the period 2015-2020[2] identifies the source of its main deficiencies by reference

---

[1] Cosmin Soare-Filatov, lawyer with the Bucharest Bar Association, Romania, csoarefilatov@lddp.ro.

[2] The national strategy in the field of public procurement 2015-2020, adopted by Government Decision no. 901 of October 27, 2015, published in the Official Gazette of Romania no. 881 of November 25, 2015. The strategy is also available electronically

to the legislative framework and related practices for the reference period 2006-2015. The following aspects are mentioned: (i) the general approach in which the emphasis falls primarily on compliance with the letter of the law, rather than on merit, compounded by the insufficient expertise of the contracting authorities; (ii) the existence of a normative framework characterized by legislative inflation and that is also excessively detailed; (iii) the existence of a small number of guides and instructional texts containing useful guidance for contracting authorities and economic operators; (iv) the incidence of normative acts at the level of primary legislation containing provisions that contravene European Union directives on the matter[3]; (v) the absence of systematic analysis and constant monitoring of the case law of the Court of Justice of the European Union; and (vi) limiting of the role of the National Authority for the Regulation and Monitoring of Public Procurement as a regulatory institution and as a body for the elaboration of legislation in this matter.

At the legislative level, 2016 saw the adoption of a new package of laws in the field of public procurement[4] in order to ensure the proper

---

at http://anap.gov.ro/web/wp-content/uploads/2015/12/Strategia-Nationala-Achizitii-Publice-final.pdf, accessed October 1-30, 2019.

[3] In this respect, see the Law on community services of public utilities no. 51/2006, according to which the management of public services treated by the law (e.g. public lighting, waste collection, water supply, etc.) can be delegated to a third party through a "delegation contract for operating activities". However, from the perspective of European legislation on public procurement, delegated contracts should fall into either the category of public procurement contracts or concessions, the law in question creating a parallel set of rules for the award of public utility contracts. Also, see Emergency Ordinance no. 51/2014 for amending and supplementing Emergency Ordinance no. 34/2006 regarding the award of public procurement contracts, public concession contracts, and service concession contracts. This modification imposed a guarantee of good conduct, resulting in a considerable decrease in the number of appeals, without, however, establishing a direct and objective link with the decrease in the number of abusive appeals. Moreover, the automatic retention of the guarantee based on alleged damage caused to the contracting authority was declared unconstitutional by Decision no. 5/2015 of the Constitutional Court.

[4] Law no. 98/2016 regarding public procurement, published in the Official Gazette no. 390 dated May 23, 2016; Law no. 99/2016 on sectoral acquisitions, published in the Official Gazette no. 391 dated May 23, 2016; Law no. 100/2016 on works concessions and service concessions, published in the Official Gazette no. 392 of May 23, 2016; Law no. 101/2016 on remedies regarding the award of public procurement contracts, sectoral contracts, and works concession and service concession contracts, as well as the organization and functioning of the National Council for Solving Complaints, published in the Official Monitor no. 393 of May

translation of the European directives in this field into domestic law[5].

Given the theoretical and practical dimensions of the legislative intervention, its analysis cannot be included in a study such as this. For this reason, we have chosen to focus on concrete, individual situations as regards the interpretation and application of the new regulations.

In this way, we will identify the possibility of correcting one of the main deficiencies. We refer to the first deficiency noted above, regarding the general approach of the contracting authorities with a focus primarily on compliance with the letter of the law, compounded by insufficient expertise.

As was noted in the content of the strategy document exemplifying this deficiency, "in practice, the contracting authorities show a lack of flexibility and prefer a legalistic, rigid and strictly formal approach. The contracting authorities have focused their attention on the mechanical application of the regulations in force and have not pursued whether the procurement procedure reflects good practice, nor the efficiency of investment or public spending"[6].

Specifically, whether or not the good practice of the contracting authorities is respected will be referred to below. We consider those cases falling within the validity period set for offers and guarantees of participation during the award procedure, without the contracting authorities having previously requested the extension of these offers and guarantees. Such situations, apt to question the quality and interest of the participants in the procedure, have led, over time, to non-unitary and surprising solutions by the contracting authorities, by the National Council for Solving Complaints, and even by the courts.

23, 2016. On the regulation of public procurement at present see Cătălin-Silviu Săraru, *Drept administrativ. Probleme fundamentale ale dreptului public*, C. H. Beck Publishing House, Bucharest, 2016, p. 160-165.

[5] Directive 2014/24/EU of the European Parliament and of the Council of 26 February 2014 on public procurement, published in the Official Journal of the European Union L94 of 28.03.2014; Directive 2014/25/EU of the European Parliament and of the Council of 26 February 2014 on public procurement, published in the Official Journal of the European Union L94 of 28.03.2014; Directive 2014/23/EU of the European Parliament and of the Council of 26 February 2014 on public procurement, published in the Official Journal of the European Union L94 of 28.03.2014.

[6] See page no. 28, point 2 of the National Strategy in the field of public procurement for the period 2015-2020.

2. Example case and relevant legal provisions

The relevant factual situation can be rendered, in the simplest terms, through the following hypothesis: during the award procedure, i.e. before the conclusion of a public procurement contract[7], the period of an offer's validity [8] or, as the case may be, that of a participation guarantee, is completed, as established by the contracting entity. Completion of the validity period leads to the loss of status to tender in the procedure.

In this context, some contracting entities claim that a lack of diligence by bidders in not extending tenders or guarantees of participation results in a situation that sees the loss of quality bidders in the procedure and of their interest regarding the continuation of the procedure. On the other hand, bidders criticize the inactivity and passivity of the contracting entities in not fulfilling their obligation to request the prolongation of the period to receive offers or, as the case may be, participation guarantees.

In such situations, can the quality or interest of the bidders involved in the procedure be legitimately questioned, especially in the case of an appeal by them? We intend to find the answer to this question and the most appropriate instrument for this is none other than the relevant case law of the National Council for Solving Complaints and the courts.

In order to facilitate the reading of this study, we present the relevant legal provisions. These include: art. 43^1 para. (2) letter b) [9], art. 171[10], art. 209 para. (1) letter a) [11], art. 255 para. (1)-(3)[12] and art. 276 para.

---

[7] On the moment of the conclusion of a public procurement contract see Cătălin-Silviu Săraru, *Contractele administrative. Reglementare, doctrină. Jurisprudență*, C. H. Beck Publishing House, Bucharest, 2009, p. 223-226.

[8] On the conditions to be met by contracting offers in the field of administrative contracts see Cătălin-Silviu Săraru, *op. cit.*, 2009, p. 133-135.

[9] b) the validity period of the participation guarantee will be at least equal to the minimum period of validity of the offer, when establishing it, taking into account the provisions of art. 276 para. (1), as requested by the award documentation.

[10] The offer is compulsory, from the point of view of the content, during the entire validity period established by the contracting authority.

[11] (1) The contracting authority has the obligation to cancel the application of the procedure for awarding the public procurement contract in the following cases: a) if only unacceptable and/or non-compliant offers were submitted;

[12] (1) Any person who considers himself injured in terms of a right or a legitimate interest by an act of the contracting authority, by violating the legal provisions in the matter of public procurement, may request, by appeal, the annulment of the act, obliging the contracting authority to issue an act, the recognition of the claimed right or of the legitimate interest by the administrative-jurisdictional route, under the conditions of this emergency ordinance.

(1)[13] of Emergency Ordinance no. 34/2006; art. 6 para. (2)[14], art. 76 para. (1)[15], and art. 85 letter c)[16] of Government Decision no. 925/2006. In terms of current regulations, we find the following correlative provisions: art. 2

---

(2) For the purposes of the provisions of para. (1), an injured person means any economic operator who: a) has or had a legitimate interest in relation to the award procedure; b) suffered, suffers, or risks suffering injury as a consequence of an act of the contracting authority, which may produce legal effects, or as a result of non-resolution within the legal term of a request regarding the respective award procedure.

(3) For the purposes of the provisions of para. (1), the act of the contracting authority is understood as any administrative act, any other administrative operation that produces or can produce legal effects, failure to fulfill within the legal term an obligation stipulated by this emergency ordinance, omission or refusal to issue an act or to perform a certain operation, in connection with or within the award procedure.

[13] (1) The Council resolves on the merits an appeal within 20 days of the date of receipt of the public procurement file from the contracting authority, respectively within 10 days in the case of the incidence of an exception which prevents the analysis of the appeal in its substance, according to art. 278 para. (1). In duly justified cases, the time limit for resolving the appeal can be extended only once by another 10 days.

[14] (2) The period of validity of a bid, stipulated in the announcement/invitation to participate and the award documentation, must be established so that it extends until the moment of the conclusion of the contract/framework agreement. When establishing the period of validity of tenders, the contracting authority will take into account estimates regarding the period necessary for the analysis and evaluation of tenders, the period required for verifications related to these activities, as well as the legal period for resolving any appeals. Without affecting the provisions of art. 93 paragraph (3) and assuming the implications of the provisions of art. 97 paragraph (4) letter b), the contracting authority has an obligation to request the extension of an offer's validity, as well as a participation guarantee, requiring extension in exceptional situations.

[15] (1) The working method of the evaluation commission is established by agreement between its members, taking into account the estimated timing of the application procedure and the period requested for the validity of offers.

[16] The contracting authority has the obligation to specify in the award documentation if the tenderers have an obligation to establish a participation guarantee. If the award documentation provides for such an obligation, then it must also contain the following information: c) the validity period of the participation guarantee, which will be at least equal to the minimum period of validity of the offer, as required by the award documentation.

para. (1)[17], art. 3 para. (1) letter f)[18], art. 8 para. (1)[19], art. 24 para. (1)[20], and art. 49 para. (2)[21] of Law no. 101/2016; art. 42 para. (2)[22], art. 130 para. (2)

---

[17] (1) Any person who considers they have had a right or legitimate interest injured by an act of a contracting authority or by not resolving the matter within the legal term of an application, may request the cancellation of the act, obliging the contracting authority to issue an act or when adopting remedial measures, the recognition of the claimed right or legitimate interest, by administrative-judicial or judicial means, according to the provisions of the law in force.

[18] f) A person considered to be injured being any economic operator who fulfills the following conditions: (i) has or has had an interest in connection with an award procedure; and (ii) has suffered, suffers or is at risk of being harmed as a consequence of an act of the contracting authority, capable of producing legal effects, or as a result of the non-resolution within the legal term of a request for an award procedure.

[19] (1) The person considered to be injured by an act of the contracting authority may notify the Council in order to cancel the act of the contracting authority, to oblige it to issue an act or take remedial measures, as well as to recognize the claimed right or legitimate interest, in terms of:

a) 10 days, starting with the day following the notification of the contracting authority's illegal act, if the estimated value of the public/sectoral procurement or concession procedure is equal to or greater than the value thresholds in relation to which the transmission is obligatory for publication in the Official Journal of the European Union of the announcements of participation, according to the law on public procurement, the legislation on sectoral procurement or the legislation on works concessions and service concessions;

b) 5 days, starting with the day following the notification of the contracting authority's illegal act, if the estimated value of the public/sectoral procurement or concession procedure is lower than the value thresholds in relation to which the transmission for publication is obligatory in the Official Journal of the European Union of the announcements of participation, according to the legislation on public procurement, the legislation on sectoral acquisitions or the legislation on works concessions and service concessions.

[20] (1) The Council resolves on its merits the dispute within 15 days of the date of receipt, under the conditions of art. 18 paragraph (2), of the file of the public procurement, the sectoral acquisition or the concession, respectively within 5 days in the case of an exception that prevents an analysis on the merits of the appeal.

[21] The appeal is urgently resolved within a term not exceeding 45 days from the date of legal notification by the court.

[22] (2) The participation guarantee must be constituted in the amount and for the validity period provided in the award documentation.

and (3)[23], and art. 143 para. (2) letter i)[24] of Government Decision no. 394/2016 (in the same sense, see also article 36 para. (2), article 124, article 137 para. (2) letter i) of Government Decision no. 395/2016).

3. The relevant case law

3.1. The opinion expressed in the sense of losing the quality and interest of bidders in the procedure

In the perspective of case law, the council and the courts have been inclined to rule that, for the expiration of an offer or, as the case may be, a guarantee of participation, the bidders are responsible and it is through their lack of diligence that they lose their quality and interest in procedure. It is considered to be a failure of the contracting authorities to request an extension of the validity period in these situations. We look at the considerations that have underpinned this solution.

In solving a complaint registered no. 16651 of June 1, 2016, the council appreciated that the contracting authority had the obligation to request bidders to extend the validity of bids in exceptional situations (such as the lodging of an appeal). Equally, however, the council held that the participants in the procedure had to do all due diligence to maintain their status as participants in the procedure, including the periodic extension of tenders.

However, from the documents in the case file, the council found that the contracting authority did not request the two bidders whose bids were declared admissible to extend their bids, and they did not extend them

---

[23] (1) The offer has a binding character, from the point of view of the content, during the entire validity period established by the contracting entity and assumed by the tenderer.

(2) The period of validity of bids, provided in the notice/invitation to tender and in the award documentation, must be established so as to cover all the stages until the time the contract/framework agreement is concluded.

(3) When establishing the period of validity of the tenders, the contracting entity shall take into account estimates regarding the period necessary for the analysis and evaluation of tenders, the period necessary for verifications related to these activities, as well as the legal period to resolve any appeals. The contracting entity has the obligation to request the extension of the validity of offers, as well as participation guarantees, in exceptional situations requiring an extension. If an economic operator does not comply with this request, his offer will be considered unacceptable.

[24] The offer is considered unacceptable if the tenderer refuses to extend the period of validity of the offer and the participation guarantee.

on their own initiative. Thus, the council noted that at the date of issuing the decision no offer was valid.

The council has shown that the issue of the validity of an offer is a priority in the analysis because if the tenderer does not extend the tender to make it valid throughout the award procedure (including the period for resolving complaints), the economic operator loses the right to be awarded the contract. The tenderer becomes a foreigner to the procedure, never having the possibility of concluding the contract forming the object of the award procedure. Thus, the fulfillment of the offer term would expire and the bidder would lose the right to be designated a winner as a result of losing the status of participant in the procedure.

According to the council, as long as the legislation in force refers to the extension of offers, it is necessary that they be valid at the reference time of the extension. Submitting a new offer cannot cover for a non-extension, being an act outside the initially submitted offer. All extensions of offers are additional acts of the initial offer. However, the council showed that the eventual admission of the contesting association could not restore a bidder's position in this award procedure, because an offer that had already expired could not be extended and there was a lack of extension of the document in question during the validity period. This proved the cessation of the bidder's quality and he could no longer have an interest in continuing the procedure, not having a valid offer to be evaluated. Moreover, even in the hypothetical situation in which the appeal could be admitted, there would be no possibility of signing the contract as long as the offer was no longer valid, an attitude that violated the law in force regarding public procurement.

In these circumstances, the council noted that the lack of active quality and, consequently, the lack of interest of the contestant, demonstrated the lack of quality of an injured person, in this case failing to fulfil the conditions imposed by art. 32 of the Code of Civil Procedure.

Similarly, the council also gave, by way of example, the resolution of the appeal registered under no. 12983 from 28.04.2016, the appeal registered under no. 6348 from 22.04.2015, the appeal registered under no. 17176 of 2013, and the appeal registered under no. 38690 of 2013.

The council maintained a similar interpretation, even if the contracting authorities requested an extension of an offer's validity, of a request made after the initial validity deadline was met. Although the bidders responded positively to the request of the contracting authority, it was held that the extension was after the initial offer had expired, meaning that the so-called extension would not be able to produce effects for the period between the expiration of the initial one and the date of the extension.

Specifically, in the resolution of the appeal registered as no. 22439 from 18.11.2015, the council noted that: (a) according to the award documentation, the validity period of the tenders was fixed until 4.10.2015; (b) on 21.10.2015 the council cancelled the procedure report issued before the expiration of the bids and ordered a re-evaluation of the bids; (c) on 22.10.2015 the contracting authority requested the extension of bids; and (d) on 23.10.2015 the bidder replied to the request and extended his offer. However, in the council's opinion, the competitor had to proceed with the extension of the participation guarantee on his own initiative in order to be able to claim the award of the contract. As seen in the aforementioned data, this does not result in the extension of the offer beyond its validity period and results in the tenderer becoming a foreigner to the procedure. It is paradoxical that, practically, through the solution adopted the council has emptied of legal effects its own solution pronounced on 21.10.2015 in the same case with reference to the respective bidder-contestant.

Through a series of court decisions, some national courts have upheld the council's solutions. Examples include: civil decision no. 1658 of November 22, 2011, pronounced by the Timişoara Court of Appeal, Administrative and Tax Appeal Section; civil decision no. 8772 of October 31, 2012, pronounced by the Cluj Court of Appeal, Civil Section II, of administrative and fiscal litigation; and civil decision no. 7967 of July 17, 2013, pronounced by the Cluj Court of Appeal, Civil Section II, of administrative and fiscal litigation.

In civil decision no. 8772 of October 31, 2012, the court emphasized that in the context of the cancellation of the award procedure, the contracting authority had no interest in requesting an extension of the validity of offers, or, if applicable, participation guarantees. In any case, even if there was some fault of the authority in omitting to ask the bidders to extend the validity of their bids, it is no less true that the bidders did not extend their bids or guarantees on their own initiative and so they did not retain the quality of participants in the procedure. As such, there was a time when the bids had expired and if the bidder did not extend the bid so that it was valid throughout the award procedure (including during the dispute settlement period), he lost the right to be awarded the contract again, becoming a foreigner to the procedure, due to the circumstance that the fulfillment of the offer term sees the expiration of the offer and guarantees. In this perspective, the court held that, after the expiration of the offer and guarantees, they can no longer be extended, the extension being able to refer only to a valid offer that has not been terminated through expiration. The same applies to guarantees.

3.2. The opinion expressed on the pre-eminence of the obligation of the contracting authority to request an extension of the validity period of offers and guarantees and not the quality of tenderers in the procedure

According to another orientation in jurisprudence, the extension of the validity period of the tenders and the participation guarantees is arranged by the bidders within the limits determined by the contracting authority through the award documentation. As long as the contracting authority itself does not fulfill its stated obligation of requesting their extension until a new date, the bidders cannot be held responsible for the fault of the authority. We look further at the considerations underpinning this solution.

By decision no. 4013 of November 8, 2013, the council held that only the contracting authority establishes the period of validity of offers and guarantees, since there is no text in the law stating that the bidders are obliged *ex officio* to extend this duration. The council underlined that such an interpretation is logical, because, in the event that the bidders *ex officio* extend the validity period of offers and guarantees, each would consider a different period of time, at their discretion, leading to the arbitrary and unequal treatment of bidders. In the case in question, with no extension of either offers or guarantees required, the council established that there was no reason to consider that the competing company had lost its status as a bidder, especially since its statements were in the opposite direction, i.e. that it still wished to participate. As such, due to its own fault in not requesting an extension of the validity period for offers and guarantees, the contracting authority could not oppose the tenderer retaining its quality in the procedure.

Similarly, the council presented decision no. 1959 from June 22, 2012, decision no. 4013 of November 8, 2013, and decision no. 716 of May 8, 2019 by way of example[25]. In essence, the decision of the council could be reduced to the fact that responsibility for requesting an extension of the validity period of an offer and guarantee of participation belongs entirely to the contracting authority and bidders can only be sanctioned if they do not comply with this request.

Through a series of court decisions, some national courts have upheld the council's solutions. For example: civil decision no. 3171 of

---

[25] The relevant literature confirms the council's solution, stressing that: "In the absence of a request from the contracting authority to extend the validity of the participation guarantee, the invocation of the contestant's lack of interest on the grounds that the validity of his participation guarantee expires without foundation". See Dumitru-Daniel Șerban, *Jurisprudență comentată în materia achizițiilor publice*, vol. IV, Hamangiu Publishing House, Bucharest, 2014, p. 221.

September 20, 2012, pronounced by the Bucharest Court of Appeal, Section IX administrative and fiscal litigation; civil decision no. 8772 of October 31, 2012, pronounced by the Cluj Court of Appeal, Section II of civil, administrative and fiscal litigation; civil decision no. 4877 of July 18, 2012, pronounced by the Oradea Court of Appeal; civil decisions no. 2256/R-CONT of October 24, 2012 and no. 1/R-CONT of January 9, 2013, pronounced by the Pitesti Court of Appeal; civil decision no. 341 of January 28, 2013, pronounced by the Bucharest Court of Appeal, Section IX administrative and fiscal litigation; and civil decision no. 367 of June 26, 2019, pronounced by the Bucharest Court of Appeal, Section VIII of administrative and fiscal litigation.

By this last decision, to which we refer given that it is the most recent, the court held that, compared to the provisions of art. 2 paragraph (1) of Law no. 101/2016, the law confers an active procedural quality on any person who is considered injured by an act of the contracting authority. The court also emphasized that, according to art. 3 paragraph (1) letter f) and paragraph (3) from the same act, the tenderer could have an interest in connection to the award procedure, as long as it was not permanently excluded from the procedure. However, an exclusion is definitive if it has been notified to the tenderer concerned and has either been considered legal by the council/court or can no longer be the subject of an appeal. As long as the bidder whose bid was rejected has appealed against the authority's acts, its exclusion may not yet be final. In this context, according to the mentioned legal texts, the challenger has both an active procedural quality and interest in filing an appeal.

Furthermore, the court held that the contracting authority is the one that must request the competing tenderer to extend the duration of the offer and participation guarantee, as with the provisions of art. 130 of Government Decision no. 394/2016. In the opinion of the court, according to this provision, the contracting authority determines the period of validity of tenders and it is also obliged to request the extension of tenders and participation guarantees if a tenderer lodges an appeal against an act of the contracting authority and the result of the procedure.

According to the court, a contrary interpretation of the indicated legal provision would be equivalent to the violation of free access to justice enshrined in art. 21 of the Constitution of Romania. In this context, the court considered the contracting authority's claims that an expired offer could not be extended or that a contract could not be concluded because public procurement legislation would be infringed. The court emphasized that no legal text prohibits the contracting authority from requesting an extension of the offer and so the procurement contract cannot be concluded in the event of admitting a challenge or of the eventual finding, after reassessment, that the offer of the contestant was compliant and admissible.

4. Conclusions to be drawn from research into the relevant legislation and case law

The case law mentioned in this chapter opposes a literal, rigid interpretation of the regulations in the field of public procurement, contradicting an interpretation that seeks to reveal the spirit of the legislation in this matter. In any case, the two solutions revealed by the practice of the courts and of the council are fundamentally antagonistic and cannot be reconciled.

On the one hand, the diligence that the bidders must show in carrying out the award procedure is held to be particularly high. The bidders have to follow the conduct of the contracting authority carefully and any shortcomings created by its possible negligence must be sanctioned immediately using the remedies provided by law. The omission of the chance to sanction the authority can lead even to the loss of a participant's status in the procedure

On the other hand, it should be noted that the bidder cannot be sanctioned for failing to fulfill an obligation that has as its premise precisely the fulfillment of a correlative obligation falling on the public authority. The loss of a right cannot, therefore, be based on the negligence of the one claiming that loss.

We consider that some issues of principle seem to have been settled by the will of the national legislature in relation to the legal provisions already mentioned in Chapter II.

Of these, first of all, we should mention that the contracting authorities have been given the obligation to establish the period of validity for offers and, implicitly, for participation guarantees. This is an obligation of result, but also an obligation of diligence, an aspect highlighted by the fact that the contracting authorities must ensure that the period established covers all the stages up to the conclusion of a contract, including the time required for the analysis and evaluation of the offers, as well as that which is necessary for the formulation and settlement of remedies against the acts of the contracting authority. The explanation is easy to understand, with the purpose of any public procurement procedure being to award the contract in accordance with the principle of legality and to identify the tenderer who will actually perform the public works or services covered by the procedure.

Secondly, the exercise of the obligation of the contracting authorities to set the term of validity of the tenders and guarantees of participation cannot be arbitrary, as previously mentioned. If the initial term of validity proves to be insufficient, the authority has a duty to extend it to ensure that this period is sufficient to cover the conclusion of the contract. By implication, this obligation responds to the right of access to justice and having an effective judicial remedy for bidders who cannot be denied the right to request the council or the courts analyze the documents of the contracting authority. A contrary interpretation might lead to the annihilation of this right. Imagine, for example, if a contracting authority transmitted the result of the award procedure on the day that the initial term of validity for offers expired. Following the logic expressed in the first opinion mentioned in this chapter, it would appear that the formulation by a bidder of an appeal on the same day should be rejected as being formulated by an economic operator who has no quality or interest, as long as any solution would not be able to take advantage of it as a result of the expiry of its offer and the loss of quality in the procedure.

Thirdly, the legislature has set clear deadlines for the resolution by the council and the courts of possible appeals against the acts of contracting authorities, which can support it in determining or, if necessary, extending the period of validity of tenders and participation guarantees.

Fourthly, it cannot be ignored that bidders actually have the capacity of respondents to an invitation by a public authority to participate in a procurement procedure. If the public authority is the one that sets the conditions for the procedure to be carried out, therefore including the validity of the tenders, it turns out that non-fulfillment by bidders of unforeseen extension obligations in the award documentation cannot be imputed to them.

Fifthly, the offer is an expression of a tenderer's desire to participate in the procedure. His refusal to participate in the procedure cannot be presumed, but is the result of an expression of will. As the tenderer has responded to the public "invitation" to participate in the procedure, so he can decide to keep his offer after the initial period only if such an invitation is clearly and concretely formulated. The will of the contracting authority can, therefore, limit the right of the tenderer to participate in the procedure, only in compliance with the principle of legality, within the express limits provided by law, in cases of rejection of an offer (as non-compliant, unacceptable, or through a refusal to extend), not contested by the tenderer or, as the case may be, confirmed by the council and/or the court.

The aforementioned elements of the principle, resulting from an interpretation of the current regulations in this field and shared by an important part of the national case law, seem to correspond to the requirements of the National Strategy in the field of public procurement. However, as reflected in some of the case law corresponding to the previous regulations, we can conclude that the progress made consists in the greater precision and clarity of the relevant provisions. This progress, however, will inevitably lead to the more clarity in interpretation and a unitary practice.

Bibliography

1. Cătălin-Silviu Săraru, *Contractele administrative. Reglementare, doctrină. Jurisprudență*, C. H. Beck Publishing House, Bucharest, 2009.
2. Cătălin-Silviu Săraru, *Drept administrativ. Probleme fundamentale ale dreptului public*, C. H. Beck Publishing House, Bucharest, 2016.
3. Dumitru-Daniel Șerban, *Jurisprudență comentată în materia achizițiilor publice,* vol. IV, Hamangiu Publishing House, Bucharest, 2014.
4. Law no. 98/2016 regarding public procurement, published in the Official Gazette no. 390 dated May 23, 2016.
5. Law no. 99/2016 on sectoral acquisitions, published in the Official Gazette no. 391 dated May 23, 2016.
6. Law no. 100/2016 on works concessions and service concessions, published in the Official Gazette no. 392 of May 23, 2016.
7. Law no. 101/2016 on remedies regarding the award of public procurement contracts, sectoral contracts, and works concession and service concession contracts, as well as for the organization and functioning of the National Council for Solving Complaints, published in the Official Monitor no. 393 of May 23, 2016.

CHALLENGES AND PERSPECTIVES ON THE EVOLUTION OF ROMANIAN ADMINISTRATIVE LITIGATION

ASSOCIATE PROFESSOR CĂTĂLIN-SILVIU SĂRARU[1]

Abstract: *The study presented here analyzes the current situation of administrative litigation in Romania, highlighting the causes that have driven an exponential increase in the number of disputes in this field. The evolutionary prospects of Romanian administrative litigation are investigated and solutions are provided for speedily resolving the increasing number of disputes. The proposed solutions include: the adoption of an administrative procedure code; the creation of administrative-fiscal tribunals; the creation of specialized administrative jurisdictions; and the strengthening of the role of the People's Advocate through the greater involvement of this institution in verifying how public authorities comply with the law and the resolution of disputes about administrative contracts by arbitration. The importance of this research lies in its focus on how administrative disputes are regulated in Romania. This is held to reflect Romania's degree of democratization and the extent to which legal guarantees are made available to citizens in order to defend themselves against abuses by public authorities.*

Keywords: *administrative litigation, administrative courts, transparency, arbitration, public authorities, administrative law.*

JEL Classification: K23, K41

[1] Cătălin-Silviu Săraru, Department of Law, Bucharest University of Economic Studies, Romania, catalinsararu@ase.ro.

1. Introductory considerations

Constantin G. Rarincescu, in his foreword to the first Romanian monograph dedicated to administrative litigation, considers that "*the institution of administrative litigation, like most of the legal institutions of today's society, is based on two fundamental principles of any civilized state: on the principle of respecting the legal rights acquired and on the principle of the obligation of the State to ensure the proper execution of judgments*"[2]. These principles are more important than ever today.

We appreciate that, at present, guaranteeing the observance of Rarincescu's two principles cannot be achieved without better correlation between the procedural rules of administrative litigation and the norms of material law that regulate the activity of public administration.

Today, those needs of a company that must be met by public administration authorities are multiplying at a greater pace, new public services and activities are appearing, and demands for higher standards are increasing. In the face of these twenty-first century challenges, public authorities must have the legislative instruments available to enforce the fundamental rights of citizens in their work. These legislative instruments must ensure the transparency and efficiency of the functioning of the public administration and create guarantees of compliance with the provisions of art. 16 paragraph (1) of the constitution, which declares that "*citizens are equal before the law and the public authorities, with no privileges and with no discrimination*".

2. The current situation

In Romania today, we find that the number of administrative litigations has increased exponentially year on year. For example, of the total new cases registered in the courts in 2017, 32 % were in the area of administrative and fiscal litigation representing 162,195 files. This is 22,788 files more than in 2016 and represents an increase of 16.35 %.

Among the factors determining this increase in the amount of administrative litigation, we consider the following:

- Greater diversity in the needs of companies that must be met by the public administration and which determine the regulation of new activities of public authorities, and where disputes regarding them are to be solved in the administrative litigation courts.

---

[2] See C. G. Rarincescu, *Contenciosul administrativ român*, 2nd edition, "Universală" Alcalay & Co Publishing House, Bucharest, 1936, p. 8.

- The existence of legislative non-correlations giving rise to a non-unitary interpretation of legal provisions, in the absence of an administrative procedure code offering a unitary vision of the activity of public administration. The absence of a regulatory framework, which must include recognition of the motivation of individual administrative acts, a preliminary motivation for any decision by a public authority, and, finally, the motivation of any response to an administrative appeal, may give rise to suspicions about the legality of the motivations of public authorities, triggering the mechanism of administrative litigation.

- The lack of transparency in the decision-making processes of public administration. Citizens should be informed of and be able to check at any time, online, the stage of a request addressed to a public authority. They should also be informed promptly of any information and documents necessary for substantiating an administrative decision. Increasing the degree of transparency will encourage greater partnership between the public authorities and the citizenry who will thus better understand the mechanism of their operation, informed by the necessity of respecting the public interest, and also increase confidence in the final decision made by such an authority.

The growing amount of administrative litigation also highlights greater awareness among citizens of the protective procedures provided by law against the excesses of public authorities[3] and advocates for the increased specialization of judges and lawyers in this field and for the creation of special courses on administrative litigation at law faculties.

3. Perspectives on the evolution of Romanian administrative litigation

In order to approach the unitary nature of the administrative legal phenomenon, we consider that, in Romania, it is necessary to adopt a **code of administrative procedure**, which would include two parts: a part dedicated to non-contentious procedures (being the procedures for the adoption of administrative acts and the conclusion of administrative contracts) and a part dedicated to administrative litigation.

Administrative codification, as dealt with in the literature, must ensure a unitary conceptual basis as: the rational organization of an entire specialized apparatus of public administration to increase its efficiency; the precise establishment of the rights and obligations of civil servants and of

---

[3] V. Vedinaș, *Tratat teoretic și practic de drept administrativ*, vol. II, Universul Juridic Publishing House, Bucharest, 2018, p. 152.

their responsibility for public service acts; and knowledge by citizens of their rights and obligations as subjects of legal relationships with the public administration[4].

The part of the proposed **code of administrative procedure** dedicated to administrative litigation, in our opinion, should forgo the regulatory method used by Law no. 554/2004 to assimilate, in a legal sense, administrative contracts to administrative acts (a method that gives rise to numerous confusions relating to the applicable regulation[5]) and introduce a distinct chapter dedicated to the settlement of disputes regarding administrative contracts. Such a chapter could regulate the principles underlying the arbitration of disputes regarding administrative contracts.

In order to rapidly resolve an increasing amount of administrative litigation, we believe that the following solutions may be of benefit:

a) The creation of administrative-fiscal courts equipped with suitable logistics and personnel and with judges specializing in administrative litigation to resolve disputes. We note that, although administrative-fiscal courts are mentioned in Law no. 554/2004, at present the separate sections of administrative and fiscal litigation[6] are still maintained. We note that, for some time and in some courts, the litigation of administrative litigation has been combined with civil and commercial litigation, being judged either by the *Civil, Administrative and Fiscal Litigation Section*, or by the *Commercial, Administrative and Fiscal Litigation Section* of the courts.

b) The creation of specialized and independent administrative jurisdictions, having the competence to judge disputes regarding various types of administrative act, such as administrative acts relating to the civil service, public services, and public goods, etc. This would result in greater professional specialization in solving these disputes with beneficial consequences for the quality of court documents; it would also relieve some

---

[4] I. M. Nedelcu, *Considerații privind necesitatea adoptării unui Cod de procedură administrativă cu trimiteri la instituții juridice civile*, "Revista de Ştiinţe Juridice" no. 2/2006, p. 116; M. Anghene, *Necesitatea codificării normelor de procedură administrativă*, "Revista Română de Drept" no. 11/1973, p. 62 et seq.; L. Vișan, *Necesitatea codificării normelor de procedură administrativă*, "Revista de Drept Public" no. 2/2005, p. 71.

[5] Thus, for example, the question arises as to whether, under the conditions provided by art. 3 paragraph (1) of Law no. 554/2004, the prefect can attack administrative contracts before the administrative court.

[6] Article 30 of Law no. 554/2004 shows that "until the establishment of administrative-fiscal tribunals, the disputes were solved by the sections for administrative appeals in the courts".

of the pressure on the administrative litigation courts. Of course, the person whose legitimate rights or interests have been injured through these types of administrative act will have the opportunity to choose between addressing a court or addressing the special administrative jurisdiction, under the conditions of art. 21 paragraph (4) of the Constitution of Romania—an advantage of addressing this specialized public authority is that it is free. A model to be followed is that presented by the National Council for Solving Complaints, currently regulated by Law no. 101/2016 and having the role of resolving appeals in relation to procedures for awarding contracts in the field of public procurement.

c) Increasing the role of the People's Advocate through greater involvement of this institution in verifying and tracking citizens' petitions and checking that public authorities comply with the law in the process of issuing/adopting administrative acts.

d) Settlement by arbitration of disputes regarding administrative contracts. However, we consider that, in relation to the specifics of such contracts, governed by the rule outlined in art. 8 paragraph (2) of Law no. 554/2004, through which the principle of contractual freedom is subordinated to the principle of public interest, the legislation should require that arbitrators appointed to settle these disputes are specialists in administrative law and a body of arbitrators specialized in public contracts should be created within the institution of arbitration[7].

We emphasize that, in the doctrine, mediation is presented as an alternative dispute resolution modality, but it cannot be used to settle disputes on administrative litigation because the public interest and the legality of administrative acts cannot be negotiated. Furthermore, compromise solutions are incompatible with the precision and rigour that public authorities must demonstrate in carrying out such activities[8].

Unfortunately, we may observe today that, in order to relieve the pressure on the administrative litigation courts, the legislature has opted to remove disputes that traditionally belonged to the field of administrative litigation and pass them on to common law judges. Thus, following the modification of art. 8 paragraph (2) of Law no. 554/2004 by Law no. 212/2018, disputes arising from the execution of administrative contracts are given over to the competence of common law civil courts. We believe

---

[7] A longstanding institution of in the field of arbitration in Romania is the International Commercial Arbitration Court, which is attached to the Chamber of Commerce and Industry of Romania and was established in 1953.

[8] See V. Vedinaș, V.-C. Gentimir, *Poate fi utilizată procedura medierii în litigiile generate de activitatea administrației publice? Aspecte rezultate din activitatea Curții de Conturi a României*, "Dreptul" no. 1/2017, p. 152.

that this should not be the solution in the future, because this would mean that the institution of administrative litigation would be emptied of content and we would see a return to a time that could not have taken into account contemporary diversification and social specialization, which is becoming more and more accentuated nowadays. The right of administrative litigation courts to control the legality of all aspects related to the elaboration, issuance/conclusion, and execution of administrative acts is a "keystone" of the rule of law[9]. An administrative litigation judge is one who has expertise in this field and has experience of making judgments that maintain the balance between the power relations of the public authorities and persons whose legitimate rights or interests have been injured.

A very important tool for increasing the speed and ease of administering evidence in administrative litigation disputes is greater computerization, with the creation of an *online folder* system so that the relevant parties can submit and consult all documents in a case file online using an access code. The development of a *videoconferencing system* for hearing witnesses and experts etc. would also assist the process. Also, at the level of the administrative litigation courts, it is necessary to increase transparency by publishing all court decisions online.

4. Conclusions

Finally, we wish to mention that the way in which administrative litigation in Romania is regulated reflects the degree of democratization in the country and the extent to which legal guarantees are available to the citizenry in order to defend against abuses by public authorities. The regulation of administrative litigation must see the setting up of specialized courts with clear procedural rules that are capable of handling the procedural rights of the litigating parties, having as its final aim the protection of people's rights where they have been violated by illegal administrative acts[10].

---

[9] V. I. Prisăcaru, *Contenciosul administrativ român*, 2nd edition, All Beck Publishing House, Bucharest, 1998, p. 248.

[10] V. Vedinaş, L. Vişan, D. I. Pasăre, *Argumentare juridică europeană în favoarea necesității modificării Legii contenciosului administrativ. Succintă prezentare a Legii nr. 262/2007*, "Revista de Drept Public" no. 3/2007, p. 77, 78.

Bibliography

1. C. G. Rarincescu, *Contenciosul administrativ român*, 2nd edition, "Universală" Alcalay & Co Publishing House., Bucharest, 1936.
2. I. M. Nedelcu, *Consideraţii privind necesitatea adoptării unui Cod de procedură administrativă cu trimiteri la instituţii juridice civile*, "Revista de Ştiinţe Juridice" no. 2/2006.
3. L. Vişan, *Necesitatea codificării normelor de procedură administrativă*, "Revista de Drept Public" no. 2/2005.
4. M. Anghene, *Necesitatea codificării normelor de procedură administrativă*, "Revista Română de Drept" no. 11/1973.
5. V. I. Prisăcaru, *Contenciosul administrativ român*, 2nd edition, All Beck Publishing House, Bucharest, 1998.
6. V. Vedinaş, L. Vişan, D. I. Pasăre, *Argumentare juridică europeană în favoarea necesităţii modificării Legii contenciosului administrativ. Succintă prezentare a Legii nr. 262/2007*, "Revista de Drept Public" no. 3/2007.
7. V. Vedinaş, *Tratat teoretic şi practic de drept administrativ*, vol. II, Universul Juridic Publishing House, Bucharest, 2018.
8. V. Vedinaş, V.-C. Gentimir, *Poate fi utilizată procedura medierii în litigiile generate de activitatea administraţiei publice? Aspecte rezultate din activitatea Curţii de Conturi a României*, "Dreptul" no. 1/2017.

IDENTIFYING THE RIGHT OF PETITION IN THE ROMANIAN CONSTITUTION, THE MOLDOVAN CONSTITUTION, AND COMPARATIVE LAW

PHD. STUDENT CĂTĂLIN–RADU PAVEL[1]

Abstract: *This article presents some aspects regarding the right to make petitions in the context of the Romanian constitution, the Moldovan constitution, and comparative law. The right of petition is regulated by Article 51 of the Constitution of Romania. The right of petition is a fundamental right that guarantees a citizen the right to petition state authorities. This right to ask is an essential right, guaranteeing the existence and compliance of all other fundamental rights of Romanian citizens, and ensures the good administration of the state in favour of its citizens. The methods used in this study include: the comparative method, the historical method, the logical method, the sociological method, and the quantitative method. The results of this research into petition rights in the Romanian constitution, the Moldovan constitution, and comparative law are presented.*

Keywords: *the right of petition, the Romanian constitution, good administration, the Moldovan constitution, comparative law.*

JEL Classification: K10, K23

---

[1] Cătălin-Radu Pavel, lawyer of the Bucharest Bar Association, Romania, radu.pavel@avocatpavel.ro.

1. Introductory aspects

The right of petition is a fundamental right of the citizenry. It guarantees the right to make requests to state authorities[2]. This right to demand, being an essential right, guarantees the existence and respect of all other fundamental rights of citizens and ensures the good administration of the state in favour of its citizens.

The right to petition guarantees the civil liberties of the citizen.

The right to petition is part of the category of guaranteed rights, which are rights that offer legal protection and ensure the good administration of the state. The right to make a petition ensures the right of the citizen to address a public institution and receive a reply within legal terms.

The right to petition is guaranteed at European Union level by art. 44 of the Charter of Fundamental Rights of the European Union[3]: "any citizen of the Union and any natural or legal person who has his residence or registered office in a Member State has the right to petition the European Parliament".

In our opinion, the right to petition is unique in terms of its extent and the legal effects it generates. Through its effects, it guarantees all the fundamental rights and freedoms of a citizen[4].

Furthermore, in our opinion, "in relation to the right of the citizen to petition in his own name or of the legal organizations he represents, he subsists in fundamental law along with the obligation of the state through the public authorities to respond to the submitted petitions"[5].

The right of petition guarantees the good administration of the state in favour of its citizens. The right of petition of the citizen before any public authority and the correlative obligation that the notified authorities have to formulate an answer are also guaranteed.

---

[2] On the activity of solving petitions through public authorities see Cătălin-Silviu Săraru, *Drept administrativ. Probleme fundamentale ale dreptului public*, C. H. Beck Publishing House, Bucharest, 2016, p. 203-205.

[3] The Charter of Fundamental Rights of the European Union was published in the Official Journal of the European Union, Romanian edition, C83/02/30 March 2010.

[4] Pavel Cătălin-Radu, *Aspecte selective cu privire la garantarea dreptului de petiționare*, in Materials of the International Scientific Symposium with the theme: "Criminal investigation of crimes committed with violence", Association of Criminals of Romania, Bucharest, 2017.

[5] Pavel Cătălin-Radu, *Evoluția istorică a dreptului la bună administrare,* "Revista Studii Juridice Universitare", no. 1-2, Year VI, Chisinau, 2013, Research Institute in the Field of Human Rights Protection, p. 232.

2. Identification of the right to petition in the Romanian Constitutions

The **Developing Statute of the Paris Convention of 7/19 August 1858**[6], a statute that had the value of the Romanian Constitution, adopted by the Lord of the Romanian United Principalities, Alexander I, in May 1864, initially stated in article XV that: "Only the Weighting Body has the right to receive a petition and to discuss it if necessary"[7]. Following modifications, the form of article XV was: "The petitions given to the Senate, will be sent to an ad hoc commission, which will examine and report to the Government for communication"[8].

Article 28 of the **Romanian Constitution adopted on June 29, 1866**[9] guaranteed a citizen's right to address the public authorities through written petitions, being: "the right to address the public authorities through a petition signed by one or more persons, but he cannot petition on behalf of subscribers. Only the authorities have the established right to petition in the collective name"[10].

We can identify article 53 of the **Constitution of March 29, 1923**[11], which contained provisions regarding the right to petition: "Anyone has the right to petition the Assembly by means of the bureau or one of its members"[12].

The **Constitution of Romania of February 28, 1938**[13] guaranteed the right of citizens to petition, with text similar to the constitution of 1866: "Everyone has the right to address through petitions, subscribed by one or more persons, the public authorities, but only on behalf of the subscribers. Only, the established authorities have the right to petition collectively"[14].

In Title III, the fundamental rights and duties of the citizens are laid out in the **Constitution of April 13, 1948**[15], including provisions regarding the right to petition, such as article 34: "Every citizen has the right

---

[6] I. Muraru, M. L. Pucheanu, G. Iancu, C. L. Popescu, *Constituțiile Române—Texte. Note. Prezentare Comparativă*, "Monitorul Oficial" Publishing House, Bucharest, 1993, pp. 7-14.
[7] Ibid, p. 12.
[8] Ibid, p. 14.
[9] Ibid, pp. 33-66.
[10] Ibid, p. 40.
[11] Ibid, pp. 71-92.
[12] Ibid, p. 79.
[13] Ibid, pp. 97-117.
[14] Ibid, p. 101.
[15] Ibid, pp. 121-138.

to petition, as well as the right to make demands of bodies provided by law, the prosecution of any civil servant, for crimes committed during the exercise of their service”[16].

In the **Constitution of the Romanian People’s Republic of September 24, 1952**[17], adopted by the Great National Assembly of 1952, no regulations can be identified guaranteeing the right of petition.

The **Constitution of August 21, 1965**[18] proclaimed in article 34 that: “The right to petition is guaranteed. State bodies have the obligation to resolve citizens’ petitions regarding personal and public rights and interests”[19].

The **Constitution of Romania of December 8, 1991**[20], proclaimed the right of petition in Chapter 2 on rights and fundamental freedoms. According to article 47, “(1) Citizens have the right to address the public authorities through petitions formulated only on behalf of the signatories. (2) Legally constituted organizations have the right to petition exclusively on behalf of the groups they represent. (3) The exercise of the right to petition is exempt from taxation. (4) The public authorities have an obligation to respond to petitions within the terms and conditions established according to the law”[21].

In the contemporary legal system, the right to petition is regulated at the constitutional level in art. 51 of the **Romanian Constitution, revised 2003**[22]: “(1) Citizens have the right to address the public authorities through petitions formulated only on behalf of the signatories. (2) Legally constituted organizations have the right to petition exclusively on behalf of the groups they represent. (3) The exercise of the right to petition is exempt from taxation. (4) The public authorities have an obligation to respond to such petitions within the terms and conditions established according to the law”[23].

---

[16] Ibid, p. 126.
[17] Ibid, pp. 141-159.
[18] Ibid, pp. 165-187.
[19] Ibid, p. 171.
[20] The 1991 Constitution of Romania was published in the Official Gazette no. 233 of November 21, 1991.
[21] Ibid.
[22] The 2003 Romanian Constitution was published in the Official Gazette no. 767 of December 31, 2003.
[23] Ibid.

In analysing the provisions of the **2014 draft of the Law on the revision of the Romanian Constitution**[24], we can see that it contains a proposal to revise article 51—*the right of petition*. Article 51 is to be amended as follows with paragraph (1) having the following content: "(1) Citizens have the right to address the public authorities through petitions. If the fairness of the complaint is found, it must benefit all those in a similar situation, whether or not they are among the petitioners". In paragraph 4, a new sentence is added: "Failure to comply with this obligation entails immediate dismissal from the public office of the culprit, according to the law"[25].

3. Identification of the right of petition in the Constitution of the Republic of Moldova

The right of petition was guaranteed by article 52 of the **Constitution of the Republic of Moldova**[26], which states that: "*(1) Citizens have the right to address the public authorities through petitions formulated only on behalf of the signatories. (2) Legally constituted organizations have the right to petition exclusively on behalf of the groups they represent*".

4. Identification of the right of petition in comparative law

For the purposes of a comparative legal analysis, the constitutions of the following states were selected: the Constitution of Spain, the Constitution of the United States of America, constitutional acts of the United Kingdom of Great Britain and Northern Ireland, the Fundamental Law of the Federal Republic of Germany, the Constitution of the Republic of Italy, the Constitution of the Kingdom of Belgium, the Constitution of the Hellenic Republic of Greece, the Constitution of the French Republic, the Constitution of Japan, the Constitution of the Polish Republic, the Constitution of Bulgaria, the Constitution of the Republic of Croatia, the Constitution of Estonia, the Constitution of the Republic of Latvia, the

---

[24] The 2014 draft Law on the revision of the Romanian Constitution of was published in the Official Gazette no. 100 of February 10, 2014.

[25] Citizens' legislative initiative according to Law no. 189/1999: Statement of reasons for the draft law on the revision of the Romanian Consitution—citizens' legislative initiative, December 10, 2013, published in the Official Gazette, Part I, no. 100, 10.02.2014.

[26] Constitution of the Republic of Moldova, published in the Official Gazette no. 1 of the Republic of Moldova on 12.08.1994.

Constitution of the Republic of Lithuania, the Constitution of the Grand Duchy of Luxembourg, the Constitution of the Kingdom of the Netherlands, the Constitution of the Portuguese Republic, the Constitution of the Slovak Republic, and the Constitution of the Republic of Slovenia.

The provisions found in the fundamental laws of the mentioned states were analysed in terms of the form established by each state on the right of petition.

In the analysis of the fundamental provisions of the **Constitution of Spain**[27], we can see that the right of petition is guaranteed to all Spanish citizens by section 29 paragraph 1: "All Spaniards have the right to individual and collective petition, in writing, in the form and under the conditions provided by law"[28].

The right to petition was also guaranteed in the first constitution of the world: the **Constitution of the United States of America**[29], proclaimed in 1787. The first of the ten amendments ratified on December 15, 1791, which formed the Bill of Rights, deals with freedom of religion, speech, media, freedom of assembly and petition: "Congress shall make no law respecting an establishment of religion, or prohibiting the free exercise thereof; or abridging the freedom of speech, or of the press; or the right of the people peaceably to assemble, and to petition the Government for a redress of grievances"[30].

The UK has no written constitution, but rather a constitutional construct built on tradition. The **constitutional acts of the United Kingdom of Great Britain and Northern Ireland**[31] have, throughout the history of Great Britain, "made a fundamental law written in the form of a single document unnecessary, but there are a set of constitutional rules and principles that are formally expressed through a series of habits developed through case law, to which written documents and sometimes doctrine are added"[32].

In the analysis of these constitutional acts, the right of subjects to present petitions to the king is identified in the Bill of Rights (1689). Point

---

[27] E. Focșeneanu, *Constituția Spaniei*, C. H. Beck Publishing House, Bucharest, 2006, pp. 13-97.
[28] Ibid, p. 25.
[29] S. E. Tănăsescu, N. Pavel, *Constituția Statelor Unite ale Americii,* All Beck Publishing House, Bucharest, 2002, pp. 53-86.
[30] Ibid, p. 52.
[31] E. S Tănăsescu, N. Pavel, *Documente constituționale ale Regatului Unit al Marii Britanii și Irlandei de Nord*, All Beck Publishing House, Bucharest, 2003, pp. 36-100.
[32] Ibid, p. 22.

I and point 5 of the Declaration of Rights emphasize "that is a right of subjects to present king's petitions and all imprisonment and prosecution in court because of these petitions is illegal"[33].

The content of the **Fundamental Law for the Federal Republic of Germany**[34], implemented May 23, 1949, regulated the right of petition in article 17: "Every person shall have the right individually or jointly with others to address written requests or complaints to competent authorities and to the legislature"[35].

The text of article 45c regulates the petition procedure: "(1) The Bundestag shall appoint a Petitions Committee to deal with requests and complaints addressed to the Bundestag pursuant to Article 17. (2) The powers of the Committee to consider complaints shall be regulated by a federal law"[36].

In the fundamental provisions of the **Constitution of the Republic of Italy**[37], provisions identify the right of Italian citizens to submit petitions in article 50: "Any citizen may present petitions to Parliament to request legislative measures or to express collective needs"[38].

In the **Constitution of the Kingdom of Belgium**[39], the right of any person to address the public authorities is guaranteed in article 28: "Everyone has the right to address petitions signed by one or more persons to the public authorities. Constituted bodies are alone entitled to address petitions under a collective name"[40].

The right to submit petitions in writing to public authorities is also regulated in the **Constitution of the Hellenic Republic of Greece**[41] by article 10:

> "1. Each person, acting on his own or together with others, shall have the right, observing the laws of the State, to petition in writing public authorities, who shall be obliged to take prompt action in accordance with

---

[33] Ibid, p. 82.

[34] E. Focşeneanu, *Legea Fundamentală pentru Republica Federală Germania*, All Educaţional S.A. Publishing House, Bucharest, 1998, pp. 29-140.

[35] Ibid, p. 40.

[36] Ibid, p. 56.

[37] Ş. Deaconu, I. Muraru, E. S. Tănăsescu, S. G. Barbu, *Codex Constituţional: Constituţiile statelor membre ale Uniunii Europene,* vol. I, "Monitorul Oficial" Publishing House, Bucharest, 2015, pp. 811-844.

[38] Ibid, p. 819.

[39] Ibid, pp. 151-207.

[40] Ibid, p. 154.

[41] Ibid, pp. 463-542.

provisions in force, and to give a written and reasoned reply to the petitioner as provided by law.
2. Prosecution of the person who has submitted a petition for punishable acts contained therein shall be permitted only after notification of the final decision of the authority to which the petition was addressed has taken place and after permission of this authority has been obtained.
3. The competent service or authority is obliged to reply to requests for the provision of information and for the supply of documents, especially certificates, supporting documents and attestations, within a set deadline not exceeding 60 days, as specified by law. In case this deadline elapses without action or in case of unlawful refusal, in addition to any other sanctions and consequences at law, special monetary compensation is also paid to the applicant, as specified by law"[42].

In the **Constitution of the French Republic**[43], the right of petition is regulated in article 72-1:

"The conditions in which voters in each territorial community may use their right of petition to ask for a matter within the powers of the community to be entered on the agenda of its Deliberative Assembly shall be determined by statute.
In the conditions determined by an Institutional Act, draft decisions or acts within the powers of a territorial community may, on the initiative of the latter, be submitted for a decision by voters of said community by means of a referendum.
When the creation of a special-status territorial community or modification of its organization are contemplated, a decision may be taken by statute to consult the voters registered in the relevant communities. Voters may also be consulted on changes to the boundaries of territorial communities in the conditions determined by statute"[44].

The **Constitution of Japan**[45] stipulates provisions on the right of petition in article 16:

"Every person shall have the right of peaceful petition for the redress of damage, for the removal of public officials, for the enactment, repeal or amendment of laws, ordinances or regulations and for other matters; nor shall any person be in any way discriminated against for sponsoring such

---

[42] Ibid, p. 481.
[43] Ibid, pp. 639-676.
[44] Ibid, p. 661.
[45] E. Focşeneanu, *Constituţia Japoniei*, All Educaţional S. A. Publishing House, Bucharest, 1997, pp. 21-68.

a petition"[46].

The **Constitution of the Polish Republic**[47] regulates the right of any person to file a petition for the attention of the public authorities in article 63:

> "Everyone shall have the right to submit petitions, proposals and complaints in the public interest, in his own interest or in the interests of another person—with his consent—to organs of public authority, as well as to organizations and social institutions in connection with the performance of their prescribed duties within the field of public administration. The procedures for considering petitions, proposals and complaints shall be specified by statute.

In the **Constitution of Bulgaria**[48], provisions regarding the right of citizens to file petitions are found in article 45: "All citizens have the right to lodge complaints, proposals and petitions with the state authorities"[49].

The **Constitution of the Republic of Croatia**[50] guarantees the right of citizens to submit petitions in article 46: "Everyone shall have the right to submit petitions and complaints, to make proposals to government and other public bodies, and to receive answers to them"[51].

In the **Constitution of Estonia**[52], article 46 identifies the right of any person to petition state institutions: "Everyone has the right to address state agencies, local governments, and their officials with memoranda and petitions. The procedure for responding shall be provided by law"[53].

The **Constitution of the Republic of Latvia**[54] identifies the right of citizens to address petitions to state authorities within the provisions of article 104: "Everyone has the right to address submissions to State or local government institutions and to receive a materially responsive reply.

---

[46] Ibid, p. 29.

[47] Ș. Deaconu, I. Muraru, E. S. Tănăsescu, S. G. Barbu, *Codex Constituțional: Constituțiile statelor membre ale Uniunii Europene,* Vol. II, "Monitorul Oficial" Publishing House, Bucharest, 2015, pp. 296-362.

[48] Ș. Deaconu, I. Muraru, E. S. Tănăsescu, S. G. Barbu, *op. cit.*, 2015, pp. 219-256.

[49] Ibid, p. 225.

[50] Ibid, pp. 399-438.

[51] Ibid, p. 409.

[52] Ibid, pp. 553-586.

[53] Ibid, p. 561.

[54] Ș. Deaconu, I. Muraru, E. S. Tănăsescu, S. G. Barbu, *op. cit.*, 2015, pp. 8-34.

Everyone has the right to receive a reply in the Latvian language"[55].

The **Constitution of the Republic of Lithuania**[56] guarantees the right of petition to citizens according to article 33 paragraph. 3: "Citizens shall be guaranteed the right of petition; the procedure for implementing this right shall be established by law"[57].

The **Constitution of the Grand Duchy of Luxembourg**[58] stipulates in article 27 the right of citizens to petition the authorities: "Everyone has the right to address to the public authorities, petitions signed by one or more persons. The constituted authorities alone have the right to address petitions collectively"[59].

The **Constitution of the Kingdom of the Netherlands**[60] has regulated the right of citizens to address the authorities through petitions in article 5: "Everyone shall have the right to submit petitions in writing to the competent authorities"[61].

Regarding the **Constitution of the Portuguese Republic**[62], provisions identify the right of citizens to file petitions in order to defend their own rights are found in article 52 paragraphs 1 and 2:

> "1. Every citizen shall possess the right to individually, or jointly with others, submit petitions, representations, claims or complaints in defence of their rights, this Constitution, the laws or the general interest to bodies that exercise sovereign power, the autonomous regions' self-government bodies or any authority, as well as the right to be informed of the result of the consideration thereof within a reasonable period of time.
> 2. The law shall lay down the terms under which joint petitions to the Assembly of the Republic and the Legislative Assemblies of the autonomous regions are considered in plenary sitting"[63].

The **Constitution of the Slovak Republic**[64] guarantees its citizens the right of petition under article 27:

> "1. The right of petition is guaranteed. Everyone has the right, alone or

---

[55] Ibid, p. 104.
[56] Ibid, pp. 45-85.
[57] Ibid, p. 50.
[58] Ibid, pp. 96-116.
[59] Ibid, p. 101.
[60] Ibid, pp. 267-293.
[61] Ibid, p. 267.
[62] Ibid, pp. 376-473.
[63] Ibid, p. 394.
[64] Ibid, pp. 487-537.

with others, to address requests, proposals, and complaints to state bodies and territorial self-administration bodies in matters of public or other common interest.
2. A petition may not call for the violation of basic rights and freedoms.
3. A petition must not interfere with the independence of a court"[65].

In the **Constitution of the Republic of Slovenia**[66], article 45 regulates the right of petition: "Every citizen has the right to file petitions and to pursue other initiatives of general significance"[67].

In making an analysis of the Romanian Constitutions in comparative legal terms on the right of petition, similar constitutional norms can be identified in the regulation of this right, starting with the Developing Statute of the Paris Convention of 7/19 August 1858 and up to the proposed revision to the Romanian Constitution in 2014. As has been shown above, in terms of comparative law, the right of petition can be clearly identified in the constitutions of states around the world with similar regulations.

5. Recommendations and proposals *de lege ferenda*

Following an analysis of the legal regulations in Romania and the Republic of Moldova regarding good administration and guaranteed rights, we can identify some aspects that could be improved:

- The right to good administration is not expressed in the Constitution of the Republic of Moldova, even though the right to administration is registered. In our opinion, this is not a right of good administration, only covering a part of the content of this right.

- The fundamental law of the Republic of Moldova establishes insufficient guarantees of tax exemption in exercising the right to petition and as regards the obligation of public authorities to respond to petitions within the terms and conditions established by law.

- The Constitution of the Republic of Moldova establishes insufficient guarantees of the responsibility of the state and of magistrates who may exercise their function in bad faith or with serious negligence.

- The Code of good administration, annex of Recommendation CM/Rec(2007)7 of the Committee of Ministers of the member states of the Council of Europe has not been adopted and recognized in the law of Romania or Moldova.

---

[65] Ibid, pp. 499-500.
[66] Ibid, pp. 549-588.
[67] Ibid, p. 557.

We also formulate the following proposals *de lege ferenda*, which we identified following the study carried out for this doctoral thesis.

- The constituent assemblies of Romania and the Republic of Moldova should introduce into the constitutions of these two countries a new article under *Title II Fundamental rights, freedoms and duties, Chapter II Fundamental rights and freedoms*, entitled the "Right to good administration". Moreover, they should look into the possibility of recognizing a code of good administration by referencing it in the text of the constitutions of Romania and the Republic of Moldova, with its content to be designated an annex of Recommendation CM/Rec(2007)7 of the Committee of Ministers of the member states of the Council of Europe.

- We also consider that a code of good administration should be developed, in Romania and the Republic of Moldova, which could contain the provisions noted in Recommendation CM/Rec(2007)7 of the Committee of Ministers of the member states of the Council of Europe.

- Using the content of article 51 of the Romanian Constitution regarding the right of petition, we consider that the provisions not found in the Constitution of the Republic of Moldova (art. 52) regarding the right of petition, in whole or in part, could be added at its next revision. This could be done by supplementing article 52 of the Constitution of the Republic of Moldova with the following paragraphs: "(3) The exercise of the right to petition is exempt from taxation. (4) The public authorities have an obligation to respond to petitions within the deadlines and under the conditions established according to the law".

- In accordance with article 52, regarding the right of a person injured by a public authority under the Constitution of Romania, we consider that the provisions not found in the Constitution of the Republic of Moldova in article 53 regarding the right to restitution of a person injured by a public authority, in whole or in part, could be included. This could be done through revising article 53 with the following paragraphs amended and supplemented.

In article 53 of the Constitution of Moldova, the terms dealing with "legitimate interest" should be extended with the following content: "Any person injured in his/her right or legitimate interest, by a public authority, by an administrative act, or by no resolution within the legal term of an application, is entitled to obtain recognition of the alleged right or legitimate interest, annulment of the act and payment of damages". A new paragraph could be introduced: "(2) The conditions and limits of the exercise of this right are established by organic law". We propose renumbering paragraph (2) as paragraph (3), and modifying it as follows: the phrase "errors committed in criminal cases by investigative bodies and courts" should be deleted and the content modified to: "Judicial errors. The state's liability is established under conditions of law and does not remove the responsibility of magistrates who exercise their function with bad faith or serious negligence". Thus, paragraph (3) could have the following content: "(3) The State is under patrimonially liability for damages caused by judicial errors. The responsibility of the state is established under conditions of law and does not remove the responsibility of magistrates who exercise their function in bad faith or with serious negligence".

6. Conclusions

The right of petition is a fundamental right and guarantees a citizen the right to make requests of state authorities. This right to demand, being an essential right, guarantees the existence and respect of all other fundamental rights and ensures good administration of the state in favour of its citizens.

The right of petition guarantees the civil liberties of the citizen.

The right of petition has the value of a guaranteed right, representing the right of a person to notify the state through its administrative bodies whenever their intervention is required.

The right of petition, being a fundamental right, has the character of a legal guarantee, benefiting, on the one hand, from the guarantee of constitutional norms and, on the other, from the legal guarantees of subjective law.

The right of petition ensures the right of the citizen to address a public institution and receive a reply within a legally defined period.

The fundamental right of petition has been designated as having the role of a constitutional guarantee through which the effective legal protection of the citizen, as well as of their other legitimate rights and interests, are ensured.

The holders of the right of petition are citizens, individuals or groups, whether they are constituted ad hoc or organized in the forms provided by law. Persons entitled to make petitions are natural and legal persons.

Corresponding to the right of the citizen to petition in his own name or of the organization he represents, he subsists in fundamental law and it is an obligation of the state through its public authorities to respond to submitted petitions. Thus, realizing the right of petition also contributes to ensuring good administration in favour of a country's citizens.

Bibliography

1. Cătălin-Silviu Săraru, *Drept administrativ. Probleme fundamentale ale dreptului public*, C. H. Beck Publishing House, Bucharest, 2016.
2. E. Focşeneanu, *Constituţia Japoniei*, All Educaţional S. A. Publishing House, Bucharest, 1997.
3. E. Focşeneanu, *Constituţia Spaniei*, C. H. Beck Publishing House, Bucharest, 2006.
4. E. Focşeneanu, *Legea Fundamentală pentru Republica Federală Germania*, All Educational S. A. Publishing House, Bucharest, 1998.
5. E. S Tănăsescu, N. Pavel, *Documente constituţionale ale Regatului Unit al Marii Britanii şi Irlandei de Nord*, All Beck Publishing House, Bucharest, 2003, pp. 36-100.
6. I. Muraru, M. L. Pucheanu, G. Iancu, C. L. Popescu, *Constituţiile Române: Texte. Note. Prezentare Comparativă*, "Monitorul Oficial" Publishing House, Bucharest, 1993.
7. Pavel Cătălin-Radu, *Aspecte selective cu privire la garantarea dreptului de petiţionare*, in Materials of the International Scientific Symposium with the theme: "Criminal investigation of crimes committed with violence", Association of Criminals of Romania, Bucharest, 2017.
8. Pavel Cătălin-Radu, *Evoluţia istorică a dreptului la bună administrare*, "Revista Studii Juridice Universitare", no. 1-2, Year VI, Chisinau, 2013, Research Institute in the Field of Human Rights Protection.
9. S.E. Tănăsescu, N. Pavel, *Constituţia Statelor Unite ale Americii*, All Beck Publishing House, Bucharest, 2002.
10. Ş. Deaconu, I. Muraru, E. S. Tănăsescu, S. G. Barbu, *Codex Constituţional: Constituţiile statelor membre ale Uniunii Europene*, vol. I, II, "Monitorul Oficial" Publishing House, Bucharest, 2015.

A COMPARATIVE ANALYSIS OF PERSONAL DATA AND ITS PROTECTION IN THE COURSE OF BORDER PROCEDURES (UKRAINE, EUROPEAN UNION)

PHD. STUDENT IRYNA KUSHNIR[1]

Abstract: *This article presents the results of a study into the concept, scope and protection of personal data in the context of border procedures. It addresses national Ukrainian and European Union legislation, as well as legal mechanisms for the protection of personal data in the activities of the European Border and Coast Guard Agency (Frontex). The purpose of this research is substantiated by the relevance of establishing the scope of personal data collected when crossing state borders and the protection of this data. This is contextualised in terms of the activities of the Ukrainian State Border Guard Service and the need to improve the circulation of such information between border guard agencies across the European Union. Based on the analysis and comparisons made in the study, proposals beneficial to the concept of personal data (in terms of its regulation and protection) in the context of Ukrainian border procedures are formulated. The implementation of the proposed measures, both legal and organizational, will enhance the level of protection afforded to personal information while crossing the border of Ukraine, enable the improvement of the processing and differentiation of personal data by officials of the State Border Guard Service of Ukraine, and bring the execution of border procedures closer to European standards.*

Keywords: *State Border Guard Service of Ukraine, European Union, personal data, data protection, border procedures.*

JEL Classification: K23, K33, K36

---

[1] Iryna Kushnir, PhD student in the National Academy of the State Border Guard Service of Ukraine, Bohdan Khmelnytskyi, Ukraine, ikushnir010@gmail.com.

1. Introduction

Individual privacy and the protection of personal data are both priorities in contemporary society. Global informatisation and a lack of clear legal mechanisms regulating the receipt, use and protection of information about an individual can lead to its widespread dissemination, violating the balance between private and public life. After all, preserving privacy is a natural desire for everyone and the ways in which personal details are disclosed should be determined by their subject. Therefore, a priority for Ukraine, as part of its rapid development as a modern information society, is the introduction of timely and effective mechanisms guaranteeing the regulation and protection of personally-identifying information and best practices in terms of its usage.

Important components of maintaining privacy include establishing a circle of entities/people who can access data (privacy), establishing an appropriate boundary between public and personal information, and determining legitimate reasons for changing this separation. In general, identification involves matching and recognizing particular features and attributing reference data to different objects, from the known to the unknown, including to a particular person.

Today, Ukrainian legislation is seeking the development of an optimally balanced model for the recognition, consolidation, organization and security of circulating information that constitutes personal data. In the activity of the State Border Guard Service of Ukraine, the use and circulation of personal data has a multifaceted importance. Firstly, the act of crossing the state border of Ukraine is undertaken by an individual (being a citizen of Ukraine, a foreign citizen, or a stateless person); secondly, the person is excluded from the list of citizens who have been banned from crossing the state border (entry/exit), granting permission for the exercise of their right to free movement; and thirdly, those individuals who may pose a threat or risk in terms of security are identified.

The fulfilment of tasks by the State Border Guard Service of Ukraine to secure the inviolability of the state border and protect the sovereign rights of Ukraine's territorial zone and exclusive (maritime) economic zone is based on certain principles, including the "respect and protection of human and civil rights and freedoms", as well as information rights guaranteed by the Constitution of Ukraine (articles 31 and 32)[2]. The

---

[2] Конституція України: Закон України від 28.06.1996. № 254к/96-ВР. *Відомості Верховної Ради України*. 1996. № 30. Ст. 141. (ст. 31, 32) [Constitution of Ukraine: Law of Ukraine of June 28, 1996. No. 254k/96-VR. *Bulletin of the Verkhovna Rada of Ukraine*. 1996. No. 30. Art. 141. (Art. 31, 32)],

need to adhere to this principle is furthermore determined by the requirement of ensuring public confidence in the State Border Guard Service of Ukraine and its personnel.

The concept of the border procedure in Ukrainian legislation is mentioned in the context of executing first and second line checks, and only in respect of foreigners and stateless persons when entering Ukraine[3]. The first line check procedure involves the following verifications:

1) checking travel documents in order to establish their validity, the availability of a permanent residence permit, or a visa according to legal requirements;

2) the availability of information on any prohibition of entry into Ukraine and on instructions for law enforcement agencies concerning persons crossing the state border in the database of the State Border Guard Service of Ukraine;

3) noting the crossing of the state border in the travel document of a foreigner or stateless person.

The second line check procedure is conducted based on a risk analysis and assessment carried out during the first line check procedure if the authorized officer of the State Border Guard Service of Ukraine has doubts about the conditions of entry to Ukraine by a foreigner or stateless person. It is intended to:

1) establish relevant places of departure and destination and the purpose and conditions of the planned stay. If necessary, it includes verification of relevant supporting documents and an interview;

2) find out if there is sufficient financial security for the period of the planned stay and for returning to the country of origin or transit to a third country, or whether it is possible to obtain sufficient financial security legally in the territory of Ukraine.

The State Border Guard Service of Ukraine works everyday with the circulation of information constituting personal data; it is also worth mentioning the agency-level database, which includes "information on persons who have crossed the state border of Ukraine"[4]. Therefore,

---

http://zakon0.rada.gov.ua/laws/254%D0%BA/96-%D0%B2%D1%80, consulted on 16.10. 2019).

[3] Про прикордонний контроль: Закон України від 5 листопада 2009 року № 1710-VI. *Урядовий кур'єр*. 2009. № 234. ст. 9. ("On Border Control": Law of Ukraine of November 5, 2009 No. 1710-VI. *Uriadovyi Kurier*. 2009. No. 234. Art. 9).

[4] Про затвердження Положення про базу даних «Відомості про осіб, які перетнули державний кордон України»: наказ Адміністрації Державної прикордонної служби України від 25.06.2007 № 472. *Офіційний вісник*

determining the scope of collection of personal data of persons crossing the state border, protecting this data in the activity of the State Border Guard Service of Ukraine, and making proposals to improve the circulation of such information based on the practice of European Union border authorities are of particular significance.

2. The concept and scope of personal data in Ukrainian legislation

The Law of Ukraine "On Information" specifies that information about a natural person (personal data) implies information or a set of information about an individual who is identified or can be specifically identified (art. 11)[5]. Part 2 of art. 11 of this law establishes a limited list of data defining information about a person, namely: nationality, education, marital status, religious belief, and health status; as well as address, date and place of birth. The indicated norm excludes a set of basic elements of personal identification, including surname, name and patronymic. There may be other pieces of information too (e.g. taxpayer account number, bank card, etc.).

The Law of Ukraine "On the Protection of Personal Data" stipulates that personal data is information or a collection of information about an individual who is identified or can be specifically identified[6], being identical in this respect to the above mentioned provision of the Law of Ukraine "On Information". Similarly, it does not provide a specified list of types of such information. In part 4 of art. 6 of this law, the category "primary source of information about a natural person" entails: documents issued in his/her name; documents signed by him/her; and information that

України. 2007 р. №50. Ст. 2047. (On approval of the Regulation about the database "Information on persons who crossed the state border of Ukraine": Order of the Administration of the State Border Guard Service of Ukraine of June 25, 2007 No. 472. *Official Bulletin of Ukraine*. 2007. No. 50. Art. 2047).

[5] Про інформацію: Закон України від 2 жовтня 1992 року. *Відомості Верховної Ради України*. 1992. № 48. Ст. 650. ("On Information": Law of Ukraine of October 2, 1992. *Bulletin of the Verkhovna Rada of Ukraine*. 1992. No. 48. Art. 650).

[6] Про доступ до публічної інформації: Закону України від 13.01.2011. № 2939-VI. *Відомості Верховної Ради України*, 2011. № 32. Ст. 314. ("On Access to Public Information": Law of Ukraine of January 13, 2011. No. 2939-VI. *Bulletin of the Verkhovna Rada of Ukraine*, 2011. No. 32. Art. 314).

an individual provides about him/herself[7]. It can be seen that the pieces of information by which a particular person can be identified are: name, signature, and other personal information.

3. Fixing the concept of "personal data" in EU legislation

The protection of individuals with regard to personal data processing is a fundamental right established, alongside other rights and freedoms, by the Treaty on the Functioning of the European Union (TFEU) and the Charter of Fundamental Rights of the European Union; it is considered to be distinct from the right to privacy[8].

In accordance with these treaties, and acknowledging the importance of the field of data protection, the EU legislature has decided to adopt this legislation as a regulation instead of a directive. This is because, unlike a directive, a regulation is directly binding on and applicable in all member states[9].

Regulation (EU) 2016/679 of the European Parliament and of the Council of 04 May 2016, "General Data Protection Regulation", states that the term "personal data" means *any information* relating to an identified natural person ("data subject"). It specifies that an individual can be identified directly or indirectly, in particular, by reference to an identifier, such as name, identification number, location information, and any online identifier that characterizes the physical, physiological, genetic, mental, spiritual, economic, cultural or social identity of an individual. In practice, this also includes all data that are available or can refer to an individual in any way. For example, phone number, credit card, bank account, license plate, appearance, and customer number or address are all pieces of personal information; additional examples may include an IP address, opinion,

---

[7] Про інформацію: Закон України від 2 жовтня 1992 року. *Відомості Верховної Ради України*. 1992. № 48. Ст. 650 ("On Information": Law of Ukraine of October 2, 1992. *Bulletin of the Verkhovna Rada of Ukraine*. 1992. No. 48. Art. 650).

[8] See in this regard Dragoş Mănescu, *Recovery of claims in the GDPR (General Data Protection Regulation) era*, "Juridical Tribune: Tribuna Juridica", Volume 8, Issue 3, December 2018, p. 790.

[9] Marta-Claudia Cliza, Laura-Cristiana Spătaru-Negură, *The General Data Protection Regulation: what do the public authorities and bodies need to know and to do? The rise of the data protection officer*, "Juridical Tribune: Tribuna Juridica", Volume 8, Issue 2, June 2018, p. 490.

judgement or rating[10]. Therefore, personal data is any data that can specify and identify an individual; the key data in this context are "any information" that allow us to "identify a person".

As to persons who are returning to a previous location, their personal data are: first and last name; destination, departure and place of arrival; date of birth; nationality; gender; country of origin; type and expiry date of travel document; health; whether the return is voluntary or forced; and security risk assessment[11].

The following "special categories of personal data" are used in the European Union Regulation regarding the identity of a person (art. 9 GDPR), including personal data on racial and ethnic origin; political views; religious and philosophical beliefs or union membership; genetic data and biometrics; data on health status; and the sex life or sexual orientation of an individual.

The category of "sensitive personal data" is used to refer to data on ethnic and racial origin; a photo of a person (art. 49 GDPR); and health data (art. 53 GDPR). For these data, a special processing system and a higher degree of protection are stipulated in the legislation. As can be clearly seen, the same data may belong to different categories.

It should be emphasized that the EU regulation uses the unambiguous term "personal data", in contrast to the Law of Ukraine "On Information", where "personal data" is identified with the concept of "information about a natural person" (art. 11), which can cause confusion in law enforcement activities.

4. Substantiating the list of information belonging to the category of personal data

V. A. Lipkan and V. Yu. Baskakov have devised the following list of information that covers personal data: name, surname and patronymic; nationality; education; marital status; religious belief; health status; address; place of birth; date of birth; property status; racial or ethnic origin; political, religious or ideological beliefs; membership of political parties and trade

---

[10] Regulation (EU) 2016/679 (General Data Protection Regulation) in the current version of the OJ L 119, 04.05.2016, https://gdpr-info.eu/art-4-gdpr/, consulted on 20.10.2019.

[11] Data protection notice for Frontex application for return (FAR), http://frontex.europa.eu/assets/Data_Protection/Data_Protection_Notice_Returns.pdf, consulted on 20.10.2019.

unions; and health or sexual information, etc.[12].

It is worth noting that there are two other important elements that refer to personal data and identify a person—a photograph (image) and a signature. In particular, during the border control procedure, there is the process of identifying a person by matching the photo (in a travel document) with the bearer, as specified in the Law of Ukraine "On Border Control": the "identification of the bearer" and establishing that it "belongs to the relevant person"[13]. In general, during border control the process of visual identification of a person with his/her image (photo) in his/her travel document is prioritized as a basis for granting permission to cross the border. As such, a photo depicting a person's image can be attributed to the information about the individual and his/her personal data.

O. O. Serebrianyk stipulates that information about a natural person is a universal category and differentiates it into the following types of information: data on a person's private life; personal data; and communication data (metadata that includes "traffic", "location data", and "data associated with the need to identify a subscriber or user"). In addition, the researcher can also include information about racial or ethnic origin, political views, religious or philosophical views, attitudes to specific events or actions, membership of a trade union, the location of a person, and information relating to his or her health, intimate life, creativity, and image[14]. Such a broad approach to personal information reflects the European provisions that "any" information can identify a person. This approach has met with support in the views of A. V. Kardash, who notes that personal information and information about one's private (personal and family life) are fairly similar concepts. At the same time, private information does not cover all the personal information of a person, because there may be a lot of information that makes the identification of a person possible, but which is not related to his/her personal or family life. Similarly,

---

[12]Ліпкан В. А., Баскаков В. Ю., *Адміністративно-правовий режим інформації з обмеженим доступом в Україні*: монографія / за заг. ред. В. А. Ліпкана. Київ: ФОП О. С. Ліпкан, 2013. 344 с., с. 218 (Lipkan V. A., Baskakov V. Yu. *Administrative and legal regime of sensitive information in Ukraine*: monograph / endorsed by V. A. Lipkan. Kyiv: FOP O. S. Lipkan, 2013. 344 p., p. 218).

[13] Про прикордонний контроль: Закон України від 05.11.2009 р. № 1710-VI ("On Border Control": Law of Ukraine of November 05, 2009. No. 1710-VI.), https://zakon.rada.gov.ua/ laws/show/1710-17, Art. 1. consulted on 19.10.2019.

[14] Серебряник О. О., *Інформація про особу як об'єкт цивільних справ*: дис. канд. юрид. наук: 12.00.03. Івано-Франківськ, 2016. 209 с., с. 96–97. (Serebrianyk O. O., *Personal data as an object of civil cases*: Thesis of Cand. Sc. in Law: 12.00.03. Ivano-Frankivsk, 2016. 209 p., P. 96–97.).

private information may not always exist in a form that allows the identification of an individual[15].

5. Modern ways of identifying a person according to personal data

The development of modern information society and e-government has led to greater us of electronic communication technology and the use of qualified electronic signatures—currently being established in Ukraine. Electronic identification is a priority in European Union countries. In particular, a citizen of the European Union, as well as other natural or legal persons residing or having a registered office in the European Union, is entitled to have access to documents held by Frontex (the European Border and Coast Guard Agency), in cases provided for under Regulation (EC) No. 1049/2001[16]. The request, submitted electronically and sent by e-mail, shall be signed using a qualified signature in accordance with the eDIAS Regulation (Regulation (EU) No. 910/2014)[17]. However, a person can also verify his/her identity by presenting his/her ID, passport, or residence permit in the European Union[18]. This alternative, one might call it the traditional way of identifying a person in the Ukrainian information space, is still the primary one, in particular when making appeals to public authorities. For European Union countries, however, priority is now given to the modern electronic identification of a person.

The development of electronic identification in Ukraine extends the means of verifying a person by use of a BankID service card, a SIM Card (MobileID), and a biometric passport in the form of an ID card, which can provide information about bank transactions, as well as a mobile

---

[15] Кардаш А. В., *Інформація про особу та персональні дані: окремі аспекти співвідношення*, «Форум права». 2017. № 4. С. 87–92 (Kardash A. V., *Personal Information and Data: individual aspects of correlation*, "Law Forum", 2017. No. 4. P. 87-92), http:/nbuv.gov.ua/j-pdf/FP_index.htm_2017_4_15.pdf, P. 91. consulted on 10.10.2019.

[16] Regulation (EU) No 1049/2001 of the European Parliament and of the Council of Europe of May 30, 2001 on public access to documents of the European Parliament, Council and Community (OB L 145, 31.05.2001, P. 43).

[17] On electronic identification and trust services for electronic transactions in the internal market and repealing Directive 1999/93/EC: Regulation (EU) of the European Parliament and of the Council: No 910/2014 of 23 July 2014. *Official Journal of the European Union.* L 257/73. 28.08.2014.

[18] Public Access to Documents: https://frontex.europa.eu/contact/public-access-to-documents/, consulted on 19.10.2019.

number (SIM card). Such methods are very convenient, but there is another side; it is necessary to take the strictest possible measures to protect data and eliminate the fraudulent use of BankID and MobileID by third persons.

As such, the clear definition of the term "personal data" in the legislation and the detailing of its meaningful content contributes to a delimitation and clear understanding of the distinction between private and public life by all officials providing information services and this is one of the primary ways of preserving and protecting personal information. In addition, in the framework of personal data protection, it is necessary to create appropriate conditions and barriers in order to prevent the dissemination and leakage of information about individuals who became known while acceding to requests by officials of the State Border Guard Service of Ukraine.

6. Protection of personal data in Frontex activities

According to the relevant regulation, the European Border and Coast Guard Agency (Frontex) ensures the protection of personal data of individuals during their processing in the institutions, bodies, offices and agencies of the European Union. Specific provisions regarding the protection of personal data in the activity of the European Union are overseen by a personal data protection officer, as assigned in Frontex, whose main task is to ensure the independent internal application of the Data Protection Regulation.

Taking this into consideration, the general principle of the agency is to process only such personal data as is necessary for the fulfilment of tasks carried out in the public interest, on the basis of treaties establishing the European Union, the Financial Regulation, or in the exercise of official powers conferred on the agency[19] (a similar rule has already been implemented in the practical activities of the State Border Guard Service of Ukraine).

All personal data processing operations should be reported to the Frontex data protection officer and, in such cases, this information shall be entered in the appropriate register. The basic information that is entered include: data processing unit, date, reason, purpose, subjects whose personal data were processed, and categories of data processed. Keeping such a register allows for the control of factual information and ensures legal compliance of personal data processing. It is expedient to keep such a

[19] Data Protection: https://frontex.europa.eu/about-frontex/data-protection/, consulted on 19.10.2019.

register on the activities of the State Border Guard Service of Ukraine dealing with the processing of personal data.

Frontex ensures that the information collected under its authority is processed and/or is accessible only by employees of the agency responsible for such operations. Personal data is provided to third parties (contractors) only in exceptional cases and under proper supervision.

Data subjects (individuals whose data are processed) have the right to access and correct their data through a written request to the agency, or even to revoke access at any time[20].

Data subjects may at any time contact a Frontex data protection officer or data controller responsible for a particular data processing operation. Data subjects apply to the European data protection supervisor.

Frontex has the right, under the strict conditions laid down in article 48 of the Financial Regulation, to process the personal data of certain groups of returnees. In addition, Frontex has the right, under article 47 (1) (a) of the regulation, in the framework of financing, to process the personal data of persons suspected of promoting illegal migration, trafficking in human beings, or other cross-border crime, including terrorism, but only in the cases provided for. If such processing is conditioned by the interests of the public (security provisions), the fulfilment of tasks is assigned by the state to border authority officials[21].

7. Conclusions

Comparative analysis of the legislation (of the European Union and Ukraine), as well as the mechanisms of its enforcement regarding personal data and their protection, enables us to identify positive directions for the development, observance and protection of information rights in all situations, including in the context of border procedures.

The analysed provisions on the concept of personal data, their scope, and their protection in the legislation of the European Union and the Ukrainian state (in the context of this research) have allowed us to determine those current trends that will positively contribute to the fulfilment of border procedures at the state border of Ukraine. Namely:

- It is necessary to clarify at the national legislative level and to consolidate the concept and scope of personal data; more

[20] Ibid.

[21] Processing personal data for risk analysis (PeDRA), Privacy statement URL: https://frontex.europa.eu/assets/Data_Protection/ Privacy_Statement.pdf, consulted on 13.10.2019.

specifically in relation to "any" data that will identify a person.

- A distinction must be made between the categories of "information about a natural person" and "personal data".

- The position of a personal data protection official in the State Border Guard Service of Ukraine should be set up; this will direct persons who need to apply for protection of their personal data to a particular official. This will strengthen the concept of personal data protection as part of national border procedures;

- It is advisable to introduce a personal data processing register, which will provide opportunities for strengthening the control and protection of personal data.

Bibliography

1. Ліпкан В. А., Баскаков В. Ю. Адміністративно-правовий режим інформації з обмеженим доступом в Україні: монографія/за заг. ред. В. А. Ліпкана. Київ: ФОП О. С. Ліпкан, 2013. 344 с. (Lipkan V. A., Baskakov V. Yu., *Administrative and legal regime of sensitive information in Ukraine*: monograph/endorsed by V. A. Lipkan. Kyiv: FOP O. S. Lipkan, 2013. 344 p.).
2. Серебряник О. О. Інформація про особу як об'єкт цивільних справ: дис. канд. юрид. наук: 12.00.03. Івано-Франківськ, 2016. 209 с. (Serebrianyk O. O., *Personal data as an object of civil cases*: Thesis of Cand. Sc. in Law: 12.00.03. Ivano-Frankivsk, 2016. 209 p.).
3. Кардаш А. В. Інформація про особу та персональні дані: окремі аспекти співвідношення. *Форум права*. 2017. № 4. С. 87–92 (Kardash A. V., *Personal Information and Data: individual aspects of correlation*, „Law Forum", 2017. No. 4. P. 87-92), htp:/nbuv.gov.ua/j-pdf/FP_index.htm_2017_4_15.pdf., consulted on 10.10.2019.
4. Dragoș Mănescu, *Recovery of claims in the GDPR (General Data Protection Regulation) era*, "Juridical Tribune: Tribuna Juridica", Volume 8, Issue 3, December 2018, p. 789-800.
5. Marta-Claudia Cliza, Laura-Cristiana Spătaru-Negură, *The General Data Protection Regulation: what do the public authorities and bodies need to know and to do? The rise of the data protection officer*, "Juridical Tribune: Tribuna Juridica", Volume 8, Issue 2, June 2018.
6. Regulation (EU) No 1049/2001 of the European Parliament and of the Council of Europe of May 30, 2001 on public access to

documents of the European Parliament, Council and Community (OB L 145, 31.05.2001).
7. On electronic identification and trust services for electronic transactions in the internal market and repealing Directive 1999/93/EC: Regulation (EU) of the European Parliament and of the Council: No 910/2014 of 23 July 2014. Official Journal of the European Union. L 257/73. 28.08.2014.
8. Конституція України: Закон України від 28.06.1996. № 254к/96-ВР. *Відомості Верховної Ради України*. 1996. № 30. Ст. 141 (Constitution of Ukraine: Law of Ukraine of June 28, 1996. No. 254k/96-VR. *Bulletin of the Verkhovna Rada of Ukraine*. 1996. No. 30. Art. 141), http://zakon0.rada.gov.ua/laws/254%D 0%BA/96-%D0 %B2 %D1 %80., consulted on 16.10.2019.
9. Про затвердження Положення про базу даних «Відомості про осіб, які перетнули державний кордон України»: наказ Адміністрації Державної прикордонної служби України від 25.06.2007 № 472. *Офіційний вісник України*. 2007 р. №50. Ст. 2047. (On approval of the Regulation about the database "Information on persons who crossed the state border of Ukraine": Order of the Administration of the State Border Guard Service of Ukraine of June 25, 2007 No. 472. *Official Bulletin of Ukraine*. 2007. No. 50. Art. 2047).
10. Про прикордонний контроль: Закон України від 5 листопада 2009 року № 1710-VI. *Урядовий кур'єр*. 2009. № 234. ст. 9. ("On Border Control": Law of Ukraine of November 5, 2009 No. 1710-VI. *Uriadovyi Kurier*. 2009. No. 234. Art. 9).
11. Про інформацію: Закон України від 2 жовтня 1992 року. *Відомості Верховної Ради України*. 1992. № 48. Ст. 650. ("On Information": Law of Ukraine of October 2, 1992. *Bulletin of the Verkhovna Rada of Ukraine*. 1992. No. 48. Art. 650).
12. Про доступ до публічної інформації: Закону України від 13.01.2011. № 2939-VI. *Відомості Верховної Ради України*, 2011. № 32. Ст. 314. ("On Access to Public Information": Law of Ukraine of January 13, 2011. No. 2939-VI. *Bulletin of the Verkhovna Rada of Ukraine*, 2011. No. 32. Art. 314).
13. Regulation (EU) 2016/679 (General Data Protection Regulation) in the current version of the OJ L 119, 04.05.2016, https://gdpr-info.eu/art-4-gdpr/., consulted on 20.10.2019.

THE HISTORIC DECISION OF THE COURT OF JUSTICE OF THE EUROPEAN UNION ON THE OBLIGATION OF MEMBER STATES TO RECOGNIZE UNIVERSITY DEGREES OBTAINED AFTER SIMULTANEOUS STUDY

ASSOCIATE PROFESSOR TEODOR NARCIS GODEANU[1]

Abstract: *In this study, our intention is to analyze the special significance of a decision of the Third Chamber of the Court of Justice of the European Union dealing with the recognition by Member States of university diplomas obtained on the basis of simultaneous study. The problem lay in the interpretation of articles 21, 22 and 24 of Directive 2005/36/EC on the recognition of professional qualifications.[2] It was pronounced on December 6, 2018 in the preliminary referral procedure, the request being made by the State Council of Italy. The Court of Justice of the European Union has ruled for the compulsory recognition of such diplomas. We consider this a "historic" decision because it obliges Member States, whose legislation requires training on a full programme basis and prohibits simultaneous registration on two training courses, to recognize, automatically and unconditionally, diplomas obtained in another Member State and where the diploma holder has attended part-time courses, has attended several courses simultaneously, or the courses have been followed in partially overlapping periods, if the training requirements are met as provided by the directive.*

Keywords: *directive, CJEU, partial training, full programme, recognition of qualifications.*

JEL Classification: K23, K33

---

[1] Teodor Narcis Godeanu, Faculty of Legal and Administrative Sciences, "Spiru Haret" University, Bucharest, Romania, narcis@godeanu.eu.

[2] Published in OJ no. 255 on September 30, 2005, p. 22-142.

1. General considerations regarding the European Union's policy in the field of vocational education and training

In terms of education policy, the European Union acts by "*encouraging cooperation between Member States and, where necessary, by supporting and complementing their action, fully respecting the responsibility of Member States towards the content of education and the organization of the education system, as well as their cultural and linguistic diversity*"[3].

Among these policy objectives, we count **the academic recognition of diplomas of study and study periods.**

The Court of Justice of the European Union represents, in the European institutional architecture, the judicial institution of the European Union and comprises the Court of Justice, the Court of First Instance, and the Civil Service Tribunal. Two essential missions fall on the Luxembourg Court of Justice: first, **establishing the legality of legal acts emanating from the European Union level** and, secondly, **guaranteeing the unified interpretation and application of European Union law.**

In accomplishing the second point, art. 267 of the Treaty on the Functioning of the European Union (TFEU), which represents ex-art. 234 of TEC, enshrines **the preliminary question procedure**. Through this procedure, the European court collaborates with national courts, which have the status of common law courts in the application of European Union law, in order to achieve a unified application of Union law and to avoid conflicting, divergent and contrary interpretations of the principles of European construction.

From a procedural point of view, in order to achieve this objective, national courts may ask the Court of Justice of the European Union preliminary questions, seeking clarification on how to interpret certain provisions of European law and ensuring that the practice of the member state does not violate European Union law. European and domestic legislation must be kept aligned for the benefit of the union.

Such preliminary requests are answered by a decision, the content of which compels the national court in its resolution of the dispute on which the preliminary question was raised. The effects of such a decision also extend to the national courts of other member states, who are notified with an identical application.

---

[3] Vătăman, Dan, *European Union: Practical specialized guide*, Pro Universitaria Publishing House, Bucharest, 2015, p. 429.

This procedure was enshrined in articles 519-521 of the Code of Civil Procedure[4], found in Chapter II of Title III, dedicated to "*the referral of the High Court of Cassation and Justice in order to issue a preliminary ruling for the disassociation of legal issues*".

By instituting this procedure, as specified in the explanatory statement of Law no. 134/2010, *the creation of a mechanism for the unification of judicial practice* is undertaken, a role that belongs to the High Court of Cassation and Justice on the basis of art. 126 paragraph (3)[5] of the Constitution of Romania[6], as revised[7] and republished[8].

The procedure, as it is regulated, "*borrows some of the features of the preliminary ruling procedure established by European Union law, even though, as noted in the literature, the two procedures operate on different planes and pursue different objectives*"[9].

The provisions of art. 519 of the Code of Civil Procedure were subject to an unconstitutional exception, resolved by its **rejection** in Decision no. 701/2015[10]. The critique of its unconstitutionality considered that it led to discriminatory treatment between a civil trial and elements of a criminal trial. This discrimination resulted from a comparison of art. 519 of the Code of Civil Procedure with art. 475 of the Code of Criminal Procedure[11], which regulates referrals of the High Court of Cassation and Justice in order to issue a preliminary ruling for the resolution of questions of law in relation to civil and criminal matters. From this comparison, it followed that "... *the legislature, regulating the procedure of the referral of the High Court of Cassation and Justice in order to issue a preliminary*

---

[4] The Code of Civil Procedure was approved by Law no. 134/2010, published in the Official Monitor (OM) no. 485/July 15, 2010. It was implemented by Law no. 76/2012, published in the OM no. 68/January 31, 2013 and republished in OM no. 763/October 16, 2014.

[5]Art. 126 paragraph (3) stipulates that "*the High Court of Cassation and Justice shall ensure the unitary interpretation and application of the law by other courts, according to its competence*".

[6] The Constitution of Romania was published in OM no. 233/November 21, 1991.

[7] The revision of the Constitution was made by Law no. 429/2003, published in OM no. 758/October 29, 2003.

[8] The Constitution was republished in OM no. 767/October 31, 2003.

[9] Violeta Belegante in Viorel Mihail Ciobanu, Marian Nicolae (coord.), *The new Civil Procedure Code commented and annotated*, second edition, revised and added, Juridical Universe Publishing House, Bucharest, 2016, p. 1466 and footnote no. 4.

[10] Published in OM no. 906/December 8, 2015.

[11] The Code of Criminal Procedure was approved by Law no. 135/2010, published in OM no. 486/ July 15, 2010, as subsequently amended and supplemented, entered into force on February 1, 2014.

decision for the delegation of some questions of law, did not stipulate the condition of the novelty of the question of law by the provisions of art. 475 of the Code of Civil Procedure"[12]. In constituting the rejection of the notified exception, the Constitutional Court ruled that the criticism "*does not represent a true criticism of unconstitutionality ... The Court notes that the examination of the constitutionality of a text of law takes into account the conformity of this text with the constitutional provisions and principles, and not through comparing the provisions of several laws with each other, as the authors of the exception argue*"[13].

2. European Union policy in a matter that was referred to the court

The application of European policy in the field of education in relation to Directive no. 2005/36/EC on the recognition of qualifications, the interpretation and application of which was addressed in the decision of the CJEU, is the subject of analysis in this paper.

Among the considerations that led to the adoption of this directive, as contained in the decision of the CJEU, is "*the elimination, between Member States, of obstacles to the free movement of persons and services*", which "*is one of the objectives of the European Union. For nationals of Member States, this includes, in particular, the right to practice a profession, as employed or self-employed, in a Member State other than the one in which they obtained their professional qualifications...*". Recital 19 of Directive 2005/36/EC is also relevant, according to which "*Free movement and mutual recognition of qualifications of doctor, general practitioner,* ***dentist****, veterinarian, midwife, pharmacist and architect must be based on the fundamental principle of automatic recognition of qualifications based on the coordination of minimum conditions of professional training. In addition, access in the Member States to the professions of general practitioner,* ***dentist****, veterinarian, midwife and pharmacist must be conditional on the need for a certain qualification, which represents the guarantee that the person concerned has completed studies which meet the minimum conditions set*".

---

[12] Ursuța, Mircea, *Code of Civil Procedure 2017 Jurisprudence Synthesis*, Universul Juridic Publishing House, Bucharest, 2017, p. 341.

[13] The Constitutional Court is not competent to rule on the application and interpretation of the law. See in this regard Cătălin-Silviu Săraru, *Legea contenciosului administrativ nr. 554/2004. Examen critic al Deciziilor Curții Constituționale*, C. H. Beck Publishing House, Bucharest, 2015, p. 10.

3. The facts

The preliminary application was made by the Italian Council of State, in a case relating to a request made by H. P., an Italian national on March 26, 2013. He requested recognition of the title "*Doktor der Zahnheilkunde*" based on a diploma issued to him on January 8, 2013 by the University of Medicine in Innsbruck (Austria). By a Decree of May 20, 2013, the ministry recognized the title of dentist, based on the document issued by the competent authority and the College of Dental Doctors of Austria, attesting compliance with the conditions provided by art. 34 of the directive[14].

On October 16, 2014, H. P. submitted a new application to the ministry, for the purpose of practicing the profession of surgeon in Italy, requesting recognition of the title "*Doktor der Gesamten Heinkunde*" issued on August 20, 2014 by the University of Medicine in Innsbruck. Among the documents attached to the application was a written statement of the College of Physicians of Austria, attesting that the title met the criteria provided by art. 24 of Directive 2005/36 and corresponded to a diploma conferring the university degree of doctor for Austria, stipulated in point 5.1.1. of the Annex to Directive 2005/35 (paragraph 11-13 of the Court's Decision,

---

[14] Article 34 of Directive 2005/36/EC in paragraphs (2) and (3) regulates the "*Basic training of a dental professional*". Thus, paragraph (2) provides that "*The basic training of a dental professional consists in a total of at least five years of theoretical and practical training, based on a comprehensive program, comprising at least the program provided in Annex V, point 5.3.1., and carried out in a university or in a higher education institution of a level recognized as equivalent or under the supervision of a university*". Paragraph (3) provides that "*Basic training of a dental professional guarantees that the person concerned has acquired the following knowledge and skills: (a) adequate knowledge of the sciences on which dentistry is based, as well as a good understanding of the scientific methods, in particular of the principles of measuring biological functions, evaluating scientifically established facts and analyzing data; (b) adequate knowledge on the constitution, physiology and behavior of healthy and sick persons, as well as the influence that the natural environment and the social environment have on the health of human beings, insofar as these elements are related to dentistry; (c) adequate knowledge of the structure and function of the teeth, mouth, jaws and related tissues, both healthy and diseased, as well as their relationship with the general health and physical and social well-being of the patient; (d) appropriate knowledge of clinical disciplines and methods that provide a coherent picture of anomalies, lesions and diseases of the teeth, mouth, jaws and related tissues, as well as of dentistry from the perspective of prophylaxis, diagnosis and therapy; (e) appropriate clinical experience under appropriate supervision*".

Third Chamber, December 6, 2018).

Faced with this situation, the ministry found that the titles of dentist and surgeon issued by the Austrian authorities were issued to H. P. on January 8, 2013 and August 20, 2014, respectively. It was also found that the later title was issued at the end of a course of studies completed with a license in medicine of 15 months duration, considered to be less than the six years required to obtain the title of doctor as specified in art. 24 of Directive 2005/36. For the purpose of clarification, the relevant Italian ministry contacted the Austrian College of Physicians to determine whether or not the title of doctor issued to H. P. fulfilled the conditions provided by art. 24 of Directive 2005/36.

Following this request, the Austrian College of Physicians replied, on March 19, 2015, that the title was in compliance with those provisions, and H. P. began his dentistry studies on September 7, 2004, ending on January 8, 2013, and his medical studies on March 21, 2006, ending on August 20, 2014.

Despite this information, which confirmed, in our opinion, that the duration of the petitioner's studies for the two specializations exceeded the limit of six years imposed by the directive, the Italian ministry refused to grant H. P. the title he needed to exercise the profession of surgeon in Italy, considering that Directive 2005/36 did not provide that a person may undergo two courses of training at the same time.

H. P. brought an action to the Regional Administrative Tribunal of Lazio, Italy[15], contesting the ministry's refusal on the grounds that it would violate the principle of automatic recognition of the titles of doctor, as provided for in art. 21 of Directive 2005/36. In his defense, the applicant also asserted that the certificate issued by the Austrian Medical College expressly acknowledged the minimum training conditions provided in art. 24 paragraph (1) of the directive. The claim made by the applicant was admitted by the administrative court in Lazio, but the ministry appealed to the Italian State Council[16]. As grounds for appeal, the ministry, supported by the national court, cited the fact that Directive 2005/36 sets out the conditions for mandatory training and should be guaranteed by member states when granting a basic medical title. It was also mentioned that art. 24 of the directive stipulates, in particular, that the basic training programme in medicine comprises a total of at least six years of study or 5,500 hours of theoretical and practical training provided by a university or under the supervision of a university. Faced with these legal requirements, the

[15] In Italian, Tribunale Administrativo Regionale del Lazio.
[16] Consiglio di Stato, in original.

appellant noted that many of the examinations sat by H. P. would have been simultaneously taken into account for the title of both *dentist* and *doctor*. Such a procedure, recognized by the law of Austria, in the appellant's view would contravene Directive 2005/36 and imply unequal treatment and discrimination between Austrian nationals and nationals of other member states of the European Union—this would also include Italy where the simultaneous registration of two qualification courses is forbidden.

The referring court also mentioned in its submission that "*part-time training is deduced from the possibility of attending simultaneously several university courses completed with a license and raises the question whether, despite the automatic character of the reunification of professional qualifications, in the sense of articles 21 and 24 of Directive 2005/36, such training fulfills the minimum conditions provided in art. 24 and in Annex V of this Directive. In the case of an affirmative answer, this court also raises the question whether the Member State notified with the application for recognition of qualifications has the right to verify that the training acquired with partial frequency in the home Member State actually corresponds to the minimum training provided for by these provisions (paragraph 20 of the Court's Decision, Third Chamber, December 6, 2018)*".

4. Preliminary questions: content and answers of the court

On the basis of these legal premises, the State Council of Italy, as a referring court, referred *two questions* to the Court of Justice of the European Union, namely: "1) *Whether articles 21, 22 and 24 of Directive 2005/36 impose on a Member State, in which the obligation of full-time training and a corresponding prohibition on simultaneous enrollment to two university courses, the automatic recognition of degrees that are obtained in the Member State of origin at the same time or in partially overlapping periods apply? 2) In the case of an affirmative answer, whether art. 22 lit. a) and art. 21 of Directive 2005/36 can be interpreted as meaning that they nevertheless allow the authority of the Member State to which recognition is requested to verify the condition that the total duration, level and quality of that training are not inferior to those of full-time continuing education?*"

Romania. As Romanian citizens, being citizens of a member state of the European Union, Romanian doctors are allowed to carry out their professional activity in other member states. We could say that it is one of the professions most prone to seeing practitioners leave the country, and we see a real exodus of doctors with serious consequences for coverage of the health needs of Romania. We may say that doctors of Romanian nationality are some of the most important beneficiaries of Directive 2005/36.

The reality is bleak and significant legislative measures, considerably increasing the salaries of physicians and other categories of medical personnel, have been taken. It is clear that Romania is still in a difficult situation, one which cannot be repaired in only a short time, regarding the provision of medical units, especially of public ones. This is a matter of respecting the fundamental right to health protection, guaranteed by art. 34 of the constitution, as developed in Law no. 95/2006 regarding reform in the field of healthcare[22], which represents, as the doctrine describes, "*a true **code** of public health*"[23]. The Romanian legislation allows specialized training to be carried out in simultaneous periods and so we can appreciate that graduates of higher education in the Romanian medical field are direct beneficiaries of this decision of the Court of Justice of the European Union.

From the considerations set out by the Court of Justice of the European Union in the judgment, it follows that the principle of equality between member states and their citizens, who are all equally *European citizens*, is a principle that runs through the whole philosophy of European construction.

Bibliography

1. Belegante, Violeta, in Viorel Mihail Ciobanu, Marian Nicolae (coord.), *Noul Cod de procedură civilă comentat și adnotat,* 2nd ed., Universul Juridic Publishing House, Bucharest, 2016.
2. Săraru, Cătălin-Silviu, *Legea contenciosului administrativ nr. 554/2004. Examen critic al Deciziilor Curții Constituționale*, C. H. Beck Publishing House, Bucharest, 2015.
3. Selejan-Guțan, Bianca, in I. Muraru, E. S. Tănăsescu (coord.), *Constituția României, Comentariu pe articole*, C. H. Beck Publishing

[22] Republished in O.M. no. 652/August 28, 2015.

[23] Selejan-Guțan, Bianca, in Muraru, I., Tănăsescu, E. S., (coord.), *Constitution of Romania, Commentary on articles,* C. H. Beck Publishing House, Bucharest, 2008, p. 319.

House, Bucharest, 2008.

4. Ursuța, Mircea, *Codul de procedură civilă 2017 Jurisprudență Sinteze*, Universul Juridic Publishing House, Bucharst, 2017.
5. Vătăman, Dan, *Uniunea Europeană: Ghid practic de spcialitate*, Pro Universitaria Publishing House, Bucharest, 2015.